# T. S. ELIOT, POET AND DRAMATIST

*By the same author*

The Aesthetics of Modernism
Anthology of French Poetry
Art and Knowledge
Britain and France, the Unruly Twins
Collected Poems
Columbus's Isle
Contemporary French Poetry
Corsica, the Scented Isle
The Eagle of Prometheus *(poems)*
T.S. Eliot, Poet and Dramatist
France and the War
France and the Problems of Peace
The French Contemporary Theatre
Impressions of People and Literature
Landmarks of Contemporary Drama
Lights in the Distance *(poems)*
Mary Stuart *(verse play)*
The Necessity of Being
Paradoxes *(poems)*
The Poetic Drama of Paul Claudel
Realism and Imagination
Reflections on Life and Death
Reflections on the Theatre *(translation)*
Religion and Modern Society
Symbolisme — from Poe to Mallarmé
The Time of the Rising Sea *(poems)*
Twentieth-Century French Thought
White Temple by the Sea *(poems)*

# T. S. ELIOT
## POET AND DRAMATIST

by

JOSEPH CHIARI

*Docteur ès Lettres*

**GORDIAN PRESS**
**NEW YORK**
**1979**

Originally Published 1972
Second Edition 1979

Copyright © 1972 by Vision Press
Published by Gordian Press, Inc.
By Arrangement With
Joseph Chiari

Distributed in the United Kingdom, Europe and Com-
monwealth by George Prior Associated Publishers Ltd.,
37-41 Bedford Row, London, W.C.1, England.

**Library of Congress Cataloging in Publication Date**

Chiari, Joseph
  T.S. Eliot, poet and dramatist.

  Reprint of the 1972 ed. published by Vision Press, London.
  Bibliography: p.
  1. Eliot, Thomas Stearns, 1888-1965—Criticism and inter-
pretation. I. Title.
[PS3509.L43Z6492   1979]      821'.9'12      79-158
ISBN   0-87752-218-9

*To Valerie*
*with affection*

"My opinion is this: that deep thinking is attainable only by a man of deep feeling, and all truth is a species of revelation. . . ."

*S. T. Coleridge*

"Man can embody truth, but he cannot know it. I must embody it in the completion of my life."

*W. B. Yeats*

"Only when the water has flowed down river after river and reaches a broad, calm estuary or comes to rest in some backwater or a small, still lake—only then can we see in its mirror-like smoothness every leaf of a tree on the bank, every wisp of a cloud and the deep blue expanse of the sky.

It is the same with our lives. If so far we have been unable to see clearly or to reflect the eternal lineaments of truth, is it not because we too are still moving towards some end—because we are still alive?"

*A. Solzhenitsyn*

# CONTENTS

# PREFACE TO SECOND EDITION

I wrote this book six years after T.S. Eliot's death, at the suggestion of a publisher, and it is now being reprinted at the request of another. Since its publication, there have been quite a few books on the same subject; many things have been said, and many opinions have been put forward or rejected. The world has changed; I myself have changed, as part of the permanence of change. The numerous books which have been written on this subject have naturally made me aware of some of the questions I might have tried to answer, and of aspects of Eliot's work which I might have stressed or perhaps explained more fully than I have done; yet, my basic approach to the problem of criticism has not altered, and the encouragements which the present study received from some quarters which I respect, have finally led me to choose to leave it as it is, rather than to face up to the impossible task of trying to cope, here and there, with some of the queries that have been raised by well-meaning readers. To have attempted to do so would have meant writing another book, which, owing to the widening field of extant criticism on the subject, would have had to carry a greater exposition of it, but would not have been basically different from the present one, which claims to be neither an exhaustive nor a definitive study of Eliot's poetry and drama. There will always be room for different interpretations and assessments of these aspects of his work.

There have been some complaints to the effect that, because I was a friend of Eliot's, I had not been "critical" enough, meaning by that that I had not insisted enough on the weak aspects of the work I was discussing and trying to assess, and with regards to this very point, I should simply like to say, as briefly as possible, two things. The first has to do with my concept of criticism and with the role of the critic. Countless books have been written on such a subject, and my aim is not to presume to add anything new to this topic, but merely to put a kind of label upon myself and thus to let the reader clearly know, from the start, what he may expect from me. My basic approach to criticism consists in always starting from the work itself, without any *a priori* thesis whatsoever in my mind. I try to approach the work to

7

be assessed with practically the same intensity and integrated consciousness as is required in the creative act itself, for criticism is, somehow, an act of re-creation, in the critic's own affective and intellectual terms, of course. If this initial experience happens to be negative, I naturally feel frustrated and disappointed, and it stands to sense that I am not going to indulge in the sadistic task of explaining at length my frustration, or attempting to apportion blame. To try to write at length about a work with which there has been no true communion, no experience of re-creation and of self-transformation and enrichment, would seem to be as barren for myself as it is bound to be for the reader. Therefore, I only feel able to write at length about works which have illumined me and, through their impact, transformed me. Once, and only once I have been able to surrender to this aesthetic experience, do I begin to reflect upon it, and try to assess the genesis of the work, its structure, its themes, the material involved the aesthetic results of the creative imagination, and finally its aesthetic and moral worth and its place in the cannon of the author's oeuvre, in his time and possibly beyond it. This is an approach to criticism which does not favour emphasis and least of all over-emphasis, on weaknesses. I shall only say that I am as well aware as anyone of what could be termed, according to the standpoint one adopts, some of the weaknesses of Eliot's drama; I must also add that he himself said: "It is often true that only by going too far can we find out how far we can go," knew them as well, and he accepted them as part of the goal he had set himself.

This leads me to the second point I wish to make in support of my decision to leave this study as it is. I have discussed at some length many aspects of the poetry and the plays I examined, with the author himself, and although in this study I may not have been able to clearly separate the friend from the poet, it seems to me that the views recorded in it have, whatever their intrinsic worth, a kind of documentary value which could contribute something towards the overall knowledge of the poet.

These brief explanations will, I hope, help the reader to approach this study with a reasonable idea of what it is about, and also to understand my gratitude towards my publisher for reprinting it.

*The Music of Poetry,* 1942.

8

# AUTHOR'S NOTE

This book was undertaken at the request of my publisher, Alan Moore. Writing it has been a sad and painful experience, for it has caused me to spend months in continuous and close company with a very dear friend who is no longer in this world. Now that the task is over, I feel glad to have been drawn to a personal assessment of his work, and to pay tribute to a great poet as well as to a great human being.

His wife Valerie, who transformed the last years of his life, has kindly read the manuscript of this book, and I sincerely thank her for it.

I also wish to express thanks to Messrs. Faber & Faber for having kindly allowed me to quote from T. S. Eliot's works.

J.C.

# I

# THE ARTISTIC AND SOCIAL BACKGROUND

Eliot was born on the 26th September 1888. Joyce had been born six years earlier, Valéry and Proust were then seventeen years old, and Yeats, who was in his early twenties, had not yet come out of his post-Romantic, pre-Raphaelite phase. Nietzsche, Mallarmé, Dostoievsky and Tolstoy were still alive; so were, of course, Tennyson and Swinburne. It was the full bloom of the Victorian age in England, and of *la belle époque* in France, the age of Meilhac and Halévy, of Gilbert and Sullivan; and the songs of Marie Lloyd in England and of La Goulue in Paris were the rage of music-hall goers. Mallarmé still had his close circle of admirers whom he entertained regularly in his salon on the Rue de Rome, but the recondite poetry which he wrote only earned him the scorn of the bourgeois, who, engrossed in materialistic pursuits, had no time for, or interest in, the arts as revelations of disturbing truths, and preferred art as entertainment, mild ornament or decoration to well-satisfied lives. The poets and artists who did not produce the kind of commodity which the bourgeois society of the day required were purely and simply ignored and treated as eccentrics, to be tolerated, or exiled to provincial schools like the Collège de Tournon where Mallarmé was sent. Their paintings were not exhibited in official exhibitions with "establishment" patronage, but at the Salon des Indépendants, as was the case for the first impressionist exhibition in 1874.

The eighteen-eighties, the age when Eliot was born, were what can be called an age of transition. In the strict sense of the word, all ages are, of course, ages of transition. There is not a moment in the life of man, or in history, when there is

11

one single dominant attitude to life; there are always, at any time, conflicting tendencies of varying strengths which manifest themselves in society. But there are also moments when one given attitude, one set of beliefs, has such an ascendancy over the others that it seems to dominate the age, and the dissenting voices are so muted that they are barely audible. One could say, for instance, that in the age of Dante Thomistic Catholicism was clearly the dominant voice of a theocentric society in which men, by and large, ascertained the awareness of their individual existences by the strength of the ties which connected them with a living God or by the consciousness which they themselves had of their living God. This attitude to life was the dominant aspect of Western civilization and European life, and that is certainly why there existed then something which could be described as a European sensibility, which Dante represents at its best. By the time of the Renaissance and the age of Shakespeare, the all-embracing gaze of the Divine or of transcendence which enfolded all men in its light had already been fragmented; the old order and structures were coming apart, and men not only no longer relied on the light from above but, on the contrary, relied to an increasing extent on the light which surged from themselves and which prompted new conquests and guided them to new adventures. Compared with the age of Dante, the age of Shakespeare was an age of transition, of fluidity, of breaking up of barriers and widening of horizons, and the genius of the age—Shakespeare —expresses the turmoils, pathos and contrasts of light and shadows of the moment, with as much profundity and imagination as Dante had been able to display in depicting the horrors and the glory of the lives of men crawling from the pits of hell along purgatorial stairs and up the ladder of Heaven, to reach final union with pure light.

These two examples simply illustrate the very important fact that great art can flourish in ages which exhibit what one might call a unified sensibility, as well as in ages of transition, when strong conflicting forces struggle for the emergence of a new dominant sensibility. I hasten to say that sensibility, or whatever one may call the inner forces or spirituality which underlie the texture of men's actions and behaviour, is not made by artists or philosophers. It is merely revealed by them, and, by becoming part of men's consciousness through such revelations, it plays a greater and greater role in the influences—religious, economic and political—which are the shaping elements of the evolution of society. Needless to say, it takes genius to achieve such revelations, and genius's scope is in fact in direct relation to the range and depth of the social sensibility which it embraces, and to the lastingness and validity of such revelations, through time and history. To illustrate these points in a summary way, one might say that the genius of Racine reveals the dominant aspect of French sensibility and of the French genius at the moment when he lived and wrote his plays; but, even although France was then the dominant power in Europe, this type of sensibility did not, by any stretch of the imagination, embrace the whole of Europe; it was in fact confined to France, in the same way as the sensibility of Wordsworth in the Romantic age was, on the whole, confined to England. It is indeed evident that the sensibility exhibited by Rembrandt in Holland or by Bernini in Italy coincides no more with that of Racine than that of Byron coincided in its entirety with that of Wordsworth. Racine and Wordsworth exhibited what one could call national sensibilities. Shakespeare, Dante and even Byron embraced wider ranges of the thoughts and feelings of the time when they lived, and beyond. This is so, irrespective of the fact that Racine and Wordsworth are widely acknowledged to be much greater poets than Byron. In fact, it seems to me that Blake, with his vision of obliterated innocence and of the power of satanic mills of industrialism, exhibits, together with Robert Burns, a wider range of sensibility than Coleridge or Wordsworth, whatever their respective range of genius may have been.

By the end of the nineteenth century the split between transcendence and immanence, fostered by the greater and greater importance granted to reason, from Bacon to Hobbes and Descartes, had finally led to the total ascendancy of reason, and therefore to the rejection of belief, or to belief being held in dissociation from reason. This kind of development had taken place more slowly in England* than in France or in Germany, and that is why the cleavage between reason and belief, and between society and the arts, which express the true reality of life and of the society to which they belong, was far more marked in France than in England. After the great wave of English Romanticism had spent its force, by the eighteen-thirties, England, more and more industrialized, prosperous and self-satisfied, increasingly sank in the quiet waters of Victorianism. There were, of course, glimmers of discontent, anxiety and social unrest, but they were barely sufficient to cause serious ripples or to upset the rich and contented life of the Victorian bourgeois. Tennyson sought to reconcile science and poetry, and to please his reading and rewarding public with his dreams of escape and his romances of chivalry; Browning fled to better skies. Matthew Arnold sought to elevate poetry and art to the half-occupied seat of religion, replaced by religiosity; the pre-Raphaelites aided and abetted the normal escapism of their materialistic society. Dickens alone sought to expose the ills of exploitation and the suffering of industrialization and urban life.

France was in a very different situation. Revolution followed revolution—1830, 1848, 1870—and the whole series was topped by foreign occupation. Positivism, materialism, spiritualism, all sought to replace religion and a God whom Nietzsche had proclaimed dead. Art was more and more dissociated from society, which preferred pleasant, soothing, undisturbing academism to art. So, for the first time in the history of art, artists and poets were driven to form a separate caste, and to carry on their search for truth, not in accord with the wishes of society or of supporting patrons, but purely and simply according to the dictates of their genius; and it is they, of course, who express the growing unfolding of the new sensibility, which, rejected at first, naturally ends in being recognized and absorbed by society, which will go on changing and preparing new developments. Symbolism connects French poetry with the very roots of Romanticism as expressed by Wordsworth, Coleridge

---

* This was probably due to the success of the Reformation in England, and to the middle-of-the-way attitude, and tolerance, of the English Church.

and Shelley; it is, if one wishes, a kind of subterranean stream, which, having gone underground in England in the eighteen-thirties re-emerges in France, in a French climate, of course, in the eighteen-fifties, and asserts, with all the violence and the uncompromising reverence for consciousness in art of the French temperament, the truth of the new forces at work in society and history. The dream of the millennium, dangled in front of men's eyes by science, has faded away; reason, worshipped by eighteenth- and early nineteenth-century man, under the name of "l'Etre Suprême", has proved unable to master the universe, to encompass the human experience, and to infuse language with the capacity to convey to the full what man thinks or feels. Real human truth has proved to be impossible to grasp, except phenomenally, and to communicate in its entirety; it can only be suggested, hinted at, and every man must apprehend it with his own means as best he can, knowing full well that there is no truly objective truth; there is only the experience, the individual experience which has to be endlessly renewed and which is never the same. Hume had already said it, and the apostle of pragmatism, Locke, had already hinted at it. Baudelaire, Verlaine, Laforgue, Corbière understood all that, and Mallarmé went further and, since reality was beyond grasp, he abolished it and replaced it by the poetic act of abolition, which is also the act of creation, that is to say, the poet in the act of projecting himself from abolished reality towards a non-existent, denied transcendence. Thus, the poetic act is all, "le Je projeté absolu"; Nietzsche's demiurgic pride could go no further. In painting, impressionism, and cubism, born with Cézanne, sought to express the experience of the artist in terms of light and volume and, later on, the Fauves did so in terms of colours, but it was, in every case, above all a question of absolutely personal experience, the truth of which could not be referred to any material or phenomenal criteria, which were meaningless.

It was in 1907, when young Eliot, who was then a student at Harvard, wrote his very first poems, that Braque used for the first time the word "cubism". The same year, Picasso painted *Les Demoiselles d'Avignon*. Claudel had already written *Tête d'Or* and *La Jeune Fille Violaine*; on the other hand, Valéry had written only a handful of poems; it was, therefore, painting which, in France, showed clearly the colours of the new sensibility. These colours were totally incompatible with the corresponding poetic sensibility of England at that time, in spite of the *Entente Cordiale*, which had been signed and widely applauded in 1904, which was also the year of the voting of the law which separated Church from State in France. Cubism, a landmark as important in art as symbolism in literature, dominates French art, with only a temporary eclipse in the nineteen-twenties, when Surrealism briefly gained some importance in the plastic arts. Cubism, whether analytic or synthetic, is above all subjective and abstract. The painter either paints or constructs the image of his own experience, with parts of existing objects selected according to his sensibility, or he makes up his painting from geometrical shapes and figures, in order to suit his purpose and to express his own experience.

The Edwardian age in England is dominated by the poetry of Tennyson, Browning, Swinburne, Kipling, Bridges, the Georgian poets, Hardy, and, later, D. H. Lawrence. I have already touched upon the poetry of Tennyson and Browning. Swinburne's music of words was too divorced from substance and from the true underlying social and metaphysical reality to have any serious claims to originality or to a close relationship with the awakening of the new sensibility. It was a poetry which had perfected to the point of artificiality the mellifluousness and the masterly vowel music of Tennyson. Kipling and Bridges satisfied the mood of the age, and they were therefore successful; so were the poets known as the Georgians, yearly anthologized by Edward Marsh. Their poetry was essentially escapist, week-endish, imprinted with pseudo-rusticity and, above all, parochial, as if the rest of the world or the harsh problems of industrialism and the growing signs of the collapse of Western civilization did not exist. One exception must be made: the Scottish poet John Davidson, whose poem, *Thirty Bob a Week*, with its stark realism, deeply impressed Eliot, who later wrote an introduction to his poems.

Hopkins was unpublished and unknown until 1918; Hardy

and Lawrence are another matter. They were two writers of genius, and neither of them was either understood or appreciated by a society intent upon material pleasures, therefore looking upon poetry as a mild, decorative pastime, or sentimental or elegant effusions which offered a veneer of culture without in any way disturbing the self-satisfaction of blinkered readers intent, above all, upon happiness. True enough, their poetry was rather traditional in content and certainly in form, and did not show any signs of breaking new ground. Perhaps this was due to the fact that they were primarily novelists, great novelists, rather than poets, even though they are very good poets. Yeats, in spite of his visit to Paris, his meeting with Mallarmé and his reading of Arthur Symons' *Symbolism*, was still lost in the supernatural, mythological world, and had not yet found his true existential voice. Neither had his fellow Irishman, George Moore. On the other hand, the precocious genius of John Synge had already detected the current weaknesses of the poetry of his age: "The poetry of exaltation will always be the highest, but when men lose their poetic feeling for ordinary life and cannot write poetry of ordinary things, the exalted poetry is likely to lose the strength of exaltation, in the way men cease to build beautiful churches when they have lost happiness in building shapes. Many of the older poets such as Villon, Herrick and Burns used the whole of their personal life as material, and the verse written in this way was read by strong men and thieves and deacons, not by little cliques only." Eliot understood at once that he had to write not a poetry of exaltation, but a poetry of ordinary life. He was well aware that Thomas Hardy's love of the countryside and rugged honesty were not appreciated by his sophisticated, pleasure-seeking fellow-beings of "la belle époque". Besides, the pastoral scenes of his poetry and of that of the Georgians were soon going to be shattered by the violent irrationalism of the Great War, which, whatever else it did, restored realism to English poetry with the memorable war poems of Wilfred Owen, Sassoon, Rosenberg and Herbert Read.

It must be noted that, irrespective of the war poems mentioned, and irrespective of the impact of Eliot's and Pound's

17

poetry, the influence of Hardy is still felt today, in the poetry of Auden, and in that of C. Day Lewis, who does not hide his admiration for this poet, any more than D. H. Lawrence did, or, for that matter, the apostle of the new poetry, Ezra Pound. Nevertheless, the fact remains that at the dawn of the twentieth century, with the exception of Hardy and Lawrence, the poetry of England was, on the whole, what Hopkins described as "Parnassian", that is to say, a poetry which repeated old forms without any fresh substance, a poetry which was escapist, meeting the needs of a society which was, on the whole, also escapist, and which did not concern itself with the profound changes that were soon going to bring about the sensibility of the new age. The revelation of this new sensibility was undeniably the work and the achievement of T. S. Eliot. He himself has said: "Sensibility alters from generation to generation, whether we will or no; but expression is only altered by a man of genius." Eliot had genius, and therefore he could apprehend the change in sensibility, and master the means of expressing it, in terms which were appropriate to it and which, in fact, made form and content one.

Once he had finished his studies at Harvard, in 1909, Eliot, like so many Americans, took the road to Europe. American writers, scholars and artists had, on the whole, understood something which Edwardian English writers had failed to understand, in spite of the interest in French literature of Matthew Arnold, Swinburne and Arthur Symons. They had understood that artistic sensibility transcended national frontiers and that it was, by then, European. Baudelaire had been, after Goethe and Byron, the exemplar of this sensibility, and so American writers went to Europe, mostly to Paris, as the place where they could connect with their old roots and bathe in artistic trends to which they felt attuned, in the same way as Thoreau and Emerson had been attuned to Rousseau and to the basic tenets of Symbolism. They were, in fact, merely continuing a two-way traffic which had made Baudelaire, Mallarmé and Valéry look upon Edgar Allan Poe as the hero of the new age and as the archetype of the poet as artist, at war with society and condemned to seek refuge in drugs and exile in order to escape from it. Eliot followed Henry James and Ezra Pound on a road which was later taken by Hemingway, Gertrude Stein, E. E. Cummings, Henry Miller and many others. So he went to Paris and began to attend lectures at the Sorbonne in 1910. Pound, who was already in England by then, had found the English poetry scene extremely depressing. The only poet who mattered, Yeats, did not seem to be able at that moment to break new ground. Eliot did not come to Europe, or did not look to Europe, in order to find a tradition which American poetry did not possess; he looked to Europe to discover the new artistic sensibility, the sensibility which expressed the feelings and beliefs of the new age which was neither specifically English nor specifically French or Spanish, but European. It just happened that, at that moment, Paris was the melting-pot where artistic ideas were forged and evolved. That is why Picasso, Chirico, Kandinsky, Chagall, Dali, as well as Eliot, Rilke and Joyce, were in Paris, and Eliot understood that the changes in sensibility and therefore in artistic consciousness were taking place on the other side of the Atlantic and on the other side of the Channel.

There are two fundamental premises which seem to me to be basic to art. The first is contained in Hegel's belief that a poet or a philosopher can no more opt out of his age than a man can get out of his skin, though of course in the case of outstanding genius he may, and he does, transcend his age. The second premise is that a creative genius is subject to the rule of heliotropism which makes him turn instinctively towards what he needs to feed his genius, and to express it, in just as natural and spontaneous a way as the sunflower turns towards the sun. Eliot had read Arthur Symons' book, *The Symbolist Movement in Literature*, when he was still at Harvard in 1908, and this is what he says: "But for having read this book, I should not, in the year 1908, have heard of Laforgue or Rimbaud; I should probably not have begun to read Verlaine, and but for reading Verlaine, I should not have read Corbière. So the Symons book is one of those which have affected the course of my life." (*The Sacred Wood*, Methuen, 1928, p. 5.) Twenty years later he said: "The form in which I began to

19

write in 1908 or 1907 was directly drawn from the study of Laforgue together with the later Elizabethan drama, and I do not know anyone who started from exactly that point." Later on, in his lecture "What Dante means to me", delivered on 4th July 1950, he said: "Of Jules Laforgue, for instance, I can say that he was the first to teach me how to speak, to teach me the poetic possibilities of my own idiom of speech." Then he continues with the words: "I think that from Baudelaire I learned first a precedent for the poetical possibilities, never developed by any poet writing in my own language, of the more sordid aspects of the modern metropolis, of the possibility of fusion between the sordidly realistic and the phantasmagoric, the possibility of the juxtaposition of the matter-of-fact and the fantastic." (*To Criticize the Critic*, Faber, 1965, p. 126.) At the beginning of his talk he had said: "I do not think I can explain everything, even to myself; but as I still, after forty years, regard his [Dante's] poetry as the most persistent and deepest influence upon my own verse, I should like to establish at least some of the reasons for it." (*Idem*, p. 125.)

Here are, therefore, the dominant influences, or rather, since the word "influence" implies a wilful acceptance of authority and directives, one should say, perhaps, the nourishing sources, which enabled Eliot to discover, and to develop, the essential structures of his own genius. Like Picasso, who explained how much he had learned from the study of *Las Meninas* by Velasquez, or Delacroix, who explained how much he had learned from the study of the works of Poussin, Eliot learnt a lot from the study of Laforgue and from the later Elizabethans, that is to say, from what one could call the minor Elizabethans, in comparison with Shakespeare, who is placed by Eliot in the category of Dante, Homer and Virgil, whose poetry "is a lifetime's task, because at every stage of maturing—and that should be one's whole life—you are able to understand it better." (*Idem*, p. 127.)

What Baudelaire and Pascal, two deeply religious writers, meant to Eliot, we shall see later; for the moment, let us examine briefly the comfort and support which he found in the poetry of Laforgue and in that of Corbière, which act as cor-

20

rectives to the rhetoric and rant of late Elizabethan drama. Eliot was very much aware of the latent and growing despair of the age, of the lack of faith in anything, of the need to avoid the easy, stereotyped emotions of the Georgians, or the large Romantic gesture, which had ceased to have currency in an age which distrusted everything, including reason and the existence of the self. Therefore, the pessimism and irony of Laforgue and Corbière, their regular puncturing of any attempt at sentimentality, self-pity, pose or unadulterated lyricism with flashes of irony which dispelled these attitudes and turned the poet into a "Pierrot lunaire", deeply impressed Eliot and brought to him the moral support necessary to deal with his own experiences, which were those of his age.

*The Love Song of J. Alfred Prufrock*, a poem with a marvellous title, is thoroughly Laforguian. It certainly takes genius to find such a title, to say nothing of the poem itself, to which we shall return later. With this poem we have the combination of a love song, like the *Complaintes de Pierrot* or *Sombres Dimanches*, with the name "Prufrock"—a dream of a name which, strange as it may seem, truly existed in Eliot's birthplace. Laforgue provided Eliot with certain attitudes and a model for wide experiments in *vers libre*, such as had been used in the later Shakespearian plays and in the work of other Elizabethan dramatists. *Rhapsody on a Windy Night* and *Conversations Galantes* are supremely Laforguian. Corbière, with greater toughness, resilience and black irony than Laforgue, provided Eliot with the stern example of a poet who could carry his real despair with the courage, true pessimism and lack of affectation of a Leopardi. He did not romanticize death or suffering. When sailors sank in the great deep, their death was harsh, stark and tragic, without any of the attitudinizing of those whom Corbière called, disdainfully, "des marins d'eau douce". As for consumption, he, who was spitting out his lungs, knew that this was no melodramatic device to wring out sentimental tears, but a cruel reality which made his life very brief. Laforgue passed from the *Chanson Triste* and musical murmurings of Verlaine to sentiments continuously deflated by the irony born of an ever acute sense of the inanity of certain gestures and of the inability to find a steady stance. The poet or the lover of the exquisite poem *Dimanches*:

> Pauvre poète et piètre individu
> Qui ne croit à son moi qu'à ses moments perdus

—cannot truly talk of love with confidence, for he does not even know who he is. Therefore he is not going to say: "I love you"; on the contrary, he says: "J'allais me délivrer d'un 'Je vous aime' ", as if he were a clown on a stage, who is there to laugh and to be laughed at, and not to play the part of the true lover. The shadow of Laforgue certainly hovers over the first poems of Eliot. *Conversations Galantes*, written in 1909, is closely linked with *Autres Complaintes de Lord Pierrot*, and *Dimanches* and *L'Hiver qui vient* have left their mark on his early poetry written at Harvard and in France. The later Elizabethans, to whom Eliot confessed his debt, display the kind of rhetoric of contrasts of grandiloquent poses and deflations which heralds the conceits and complexities of the Metaphysicals, and which, combined with the sense of the grotesque and the self-irony of Laforgue, are the hallmarks of Eliot's early poetry.

Eliot's strong affinities with France were fully developed during his stay in Paris in 1910, when he established friendly relations with the important French writers of the day— Fournier, Jacques Rivière, Valéry and many others. That is why, writing about Jacques Rivière, he could say with reason that for many years France, for him, stood above all for poetry. He knew French poetry and philosophy, particularly Bergson's, extremely well, and he had mastered the French language to the point of being able to write good poetry in French. Many years later, talking about his feelings for French poetry in *The Criterion*, Volume 13, 1934, he said: "I am willing to admit that my own retrospect is touched by sentimental sunsets, the memory of a friend coming across the Luxembourg Gardens, in the hot afternoon, waving a bunch of lilac, a friend who was later (so far as I could find out) to be mixed with the mud of Gallipoli." This friend was Jean Verdenal, to whom Eliot inscribed his first volume of poetry. So much for those who find it possible to introduce their own mental fantasies into a moving friendship which ended in conformity with a tragic pattern that was repeated millions of times during the 1914–1918 war. For, indeed, if it is sad to die this brutal way, it is sadder not even to know where the remains lie or what has become of them. The bunch of lilac has left its mark upon Eliot's memory, as a symbol of affections sadly cut short.

Baudelaire, a more mature and profound poet than Laforgue, not only strengthened Eliot's love of irony and of the realistic aspects of life, in contrast with the imprecise and tired imagery of the Georgians; he also brought to him the love of the city, of the twentieth-century metropolis teeming with men, uprooted from their rural background and made to live in anonymous, monotonous streets and houses, all alike, and all harbouring men with similar emotions, desires and appetites. He brought to him something that Eliot's strong Puritan conscience was well prepared to receive, the sense of sin, the Pascalian need for despair, before grace could descend and illumine the soul. "Baudelaire," he said, "had great strength, but strength merely to *suffer*. He could not escape suffering and could not transcend it, so he *attracted* pain to himself. But what he could do, with that immense passive strength and sensibility which no pain could impair, was to study his suffering. And in this limitation he is wholly unlike Dante, not even like any character of Dante's Hell. But, on the other hand, such suffering as Baudelaire's implies the possibility of a positive state of beatitude. Indeed, in his way of suffering is already a kind of presence of the supernatural and of the superhuman." (*Selected Essays* (1917–1932), Faber, 1949, p. 385.) Further on he said: ". . . the possibility of damnation is so immense a relief in a world of electoral reform, plebiscites, sex reform and dress reform, that damnation itself is an immediate form of salvation—of salvation from the ennui of modern life, because it at last gives some significance to living." (*Idem*, p. 389.) And he continued: ". . . *la volupté unique et suprême de l'amour gît dans la certitude de faire le mal*. This means, I think, that Baudelaire has perceived that what distinguishes the relations of man and woman from the copulation of beasts is the knowledge of Good and Evil (of *moral* Good and Evil

23

which are not natural Good and Bad or Puritan Right or
Wrong). Having an imperfect, vague romantic conception of
Good, he was at least able to understand that the sexual act
as evil is more dignified, less boring, than as the natural, 'life-
giving', cheery automatism of the modern world. For Baudelaire, sexual operation is at least something not analogous to
Kruschen Salts." (*Idem*, pp. 390–391.) And he concluded with
the well-known words: "*La vraie civilisation n'est pas dans le
gaz, ni dans la vapeur, ni dans les tables tournantes. Elle est
dans la diminution des traces du péché originel.*" (*Idem*, p.
392.) The awareness of original sin, the possibilities of damnation are part of Eliot's foremost preoccupations; he did not
need to have them taught him by Baudelaire; they were part
of his make-up; and he recognized in Baudelaire "une âme
soeur".

Baudelaire and the Symbolists have, according to Eliot and
to many students of poetry, close affinities with the Metaphysicals. French Symbolism had healed the division between
imagination and reality heralded by Descartes, and the separation of reason from sentiments which is the bane of eighteenth-
century French poetry and which, in spite of the reinstatement
of imagination by the Romantics, is nevertheless, to a large
extent, maintained by these same Romantics. Musset's and
Lamartine's feelings remain unprocessed by reason, and that is
why their poetry—some of it stamped with imagination and
of a high order—still errs too much on the side of sentimentality. The Symbolists, with their unified sensibility, with their
sense that the world was one, reunited thought and emotions
as they reunited the various and complex manifestations of
the senses, all inextricably interrelated, as explained in Baudelaire's famous sonnet, *Correspondances*: "Les parfums, les coul-
eurs et les sons se répondent."

Eliot felt that the Metaphysicals had used the same associa-
tionistic processes and the same interrelatedness of the senses
as the Symbolists. He said: "Jules Laforgue, and Tristan
Corbière in many of his poems, are nearer to the 'school of
Donne' than any modern English poet." (*Selected Essays*, p.
290.) Talking about the famous dissociation of sensibility which

indeed set in in the seventeenth century, with the end of metaphysics, intended by Locke, and completed by Descartes, Eliot
says: "Tennyson and Browning are poets, and they think; but
they do not feel their thought as immediately as the odour of
a rose. A thought to Donne was an experience; it modified his
sensibility. When a poet's mind is perfectly equipped for its
work, it is constantly amalgamating disparate experience; the
ordinary man's experience is chaotic, irregular, fragmentary.
The latter falls in love, or reads Spinoza, and these two experiences have nothing to do with each other, or with the noise of
the typewriter or the smell of cooking; in the mind of the poet
these experiences are always forming new wholes. We may
express the difference by the following theory: The poets of
the seventeenth century, the successors of the dramatists of the
sixteenth, possessed a mechanism of sensibility which could
devour any kind of experience. They are simple, artificial,
difficult, or fantastic, as their predecessors were; no less nor
more than Dante, Guido Cavalcanti, Guinicelli, or Cino. In the
seventeenth century a dissociation of sensibility set in, from
which we have never recovered; and this dissociation, as is
natural, was aggravated by the influence of the two most power-
ful poets of the century, Milton and Dryden." (*Idem*, pp. 287–
288.) I hasten to say that, though I share with Eliot his view
about the dissociation of sensibility which set in in the seventeenth century, for me its causes were purely social and were
the result of a slowly emerging change in the attitudes of men
to religion and to reason. The seventeenth century marks the
end of metaphysics, that is to say, the end of the interdepend-
ence between immanence and transcendence and of an integrated view of life. Reason and experience become, from then
on, the only means to apprehend knowledge, and imagination
is distrusted and regarded as fantasy. Faith is still given assent,
but not understanding, and feelings are experienced as perceptions and sensations. "To love, to hate, to feel, to see, all this
is nothing but to perceive", said Hume. Descartes' reference to
the perceiver's relation with God has by now been omitted, and
man is on his own.

At the time when Eliot began to write, imagism was beginning to play a part in English poetry, and he was certainly aware of it, for he had a lively admiration for T. E. Hulme. The importance of the subconscious, with the work of William James and Freud, was also becoming part of modern sensibility. So were associationism, and the use of the internal monologue, first practised by Dujardin and later by Joyce.

In 1911, while working on his thesis on F. H. Bradley, about whose importance, together with that of Bergson, whose lectures he attended in Paris, I shall talk later, he read Dante, who had a profound and lasting impact on his thinking and writing. In 1929 he published a short study which is still the best study in English on the subject. In his 1950 lecture on Dante he acknowledged Dante's persistent influence on his work: "Certainly I have borrowed lines from him, in the attempt to reproduce, or rather to arouse in the reader's mind the memory, of some Dantesque scene, and thus establish a relationship between the medieval inferno and modern life. . . . Twenty years after writing *The Waste Land*, I wrote, in *Little Gidding*, a passage which is intended to be the nearest equivalent to a canto of the Inferno or the Purgatorio, in style as well as content, that I could achieve. The intention, of course, was the same as with my allusions to Dante in *The Waste Land*: to present to the mind of the reader a parallel, by means of contrast, between the Inferno and the Purgatorio, which Dante visited, and a hallucinated scene after an air-raid. But the method is different: here I was debarred from quoting or adapting at length—I borrowed and adapted freely only a few phrases—because I was *imitating*." (*To Criticize the Critic*, p. 128.) Dante taught him the relationship between the inferno and the hell of a modern metropolis and the art of refining language: "The task of the poet, in making people comprehend the incomprehensible, demands immense resources of language; and in developing the language, enriching the meaning of words and showing how much words can do, he is making possible a much greater range of emotion and perception for other men, because he gives them the speech in which more can be expressed." (*Idem*, p. 134.) To say nothing of the notion of a European poet to which Eliot attached great importance: "... Dante is, beyond all other poets of our continent, the most *European*. He is the least provincial—and yet that statement must be immediately protected by saying that he did not become the 'least provincial' by ceasing to be local. No one is more local; one never forgets that there is much in Dante's poetry which escapes any reader whose native language is not Italian; but I think that the foreigner is less *aware* of any residuum that must for ever escape him, than any of us is in reading any other master of a language which is not our own." (*Idem*, pp. 134–135.) It is in the essay on Dante that Eliot dealt most explicitly with the problem of poetry and belief, and as he was, from his conversion to Anglo-Catholicism onwards, a fervent believer, this is a point which is well worth examining.

Eliot maintains, with reason, that the poet's private beliefs become a different thing in becoming poetry. The corollary of this statement, extremely important no doubt, is that whatever the poet says in a poem is not necessarily his own private belief, but a belief which is part of the coherence and wholeness which is the work of art. The belief which emanates from an aesthetic experience must not be isolated, taken out of context and construed as being the private belief of the poet, because the isolation, the separation from coherence, destroys its intrinsic veracity, which is part of the whole. Eliot believed that Dante did not concern himself with thinking out the beliefs and ideas which he expounded in his poem, but simply made use of the existing Thomistic theology. These beliefs, of course, were also his own, deeply held, and the notion that he might merely have entertained them is unthinkable. But these beliefs have been transmuted into, and are held together by, the coherence and organic unity of the poem, which can and must be appreciated as poetry, and not as a statement of belief. "I deny, in short," says Eliot, "that the reader must share the beliefs of the poet in order to enjoy the poetry fully. I have also asserted that we can distinguish between Dante's beliefs as a man and his beliefs as a poet. But we are forced to believe that there is a particular relation between the two, and that the poet 'means what he says'. If we learned, for instance, that *De Rerum Natura* was a

27

Latin exercise which Dante had composed for relaxation after completing the *Divine Comedy*, and published under the name of one Lucretius, I am sure that our capacity for enjoying either poem would be mutilated. Mr. Richards's statement (*Science and Poetry*, p. 76 footnote) that a certain writer has affected 'a complete severance between his poetry and *all* beliefs' is to me incomprehensible." (*Selected Essays*, p. 269.)

To Eliot, and I fully share his view, the sense in which poetry proves a truth is, and must be, primarily aesthetic, that is to say, it is a truth which is not verifiable against facts, but a truth radiating from the organicity, the beauty and imaginative reality of the whole. "Poetry", says Eliot, "is not the assertion that something is true, but making that truth more fully real to us." That is why he is, on the whole, sceptical about expounding the exact meaning of his poetry and plays. The poet, according to him, is as much in the dark as anybody else as to what goes into the making of a poem. "He has something germinating in him for which he must find words; but he cannot know what words he wants until he has found the words; he cannot identify this embryo until it has been transformed into an arrangement of the right words in the right order. . . . He does not know what he has to say until he has said it; and in the effort to say it he is not concerned with making other people understand anything. He is not concerned, at this stage, with other people at all: only with finding the right words or, anyhow, the least wrong words. . . . In other words again, he is going to all that trouble, not in order to communicate with anyone, but to gain relief from acute discomfort; and when the words are finally arranged in the right way—or in what he comes to accept as the best arrangement he can find—he may experience a moment of exhaustion, of appeasement, of absolution, and of something very near annihilation, which is in itself indescribable." (*On Poetry and Poets*, Faber, 1957, pp. 97–98.) The reader or listener has therefore a certain amount of scope to find his own meaning, but one thing is for Eliot certain: he does not need to share the beliefs of the poet in order to enjoy his poetry. "*If* there is 'literature', *if* there is 'poetry', then it must be possible to have full literary or poetic appreciation without sharing the beliefs of the poet. . . . If you deny the theory that full poetic appreciation is possible without belief in what the poet believed, you deny the existence of 'poetry' as well as 'criticism'; and if you push this denial to its conclusion, you will be forced to admit that there is very little poetry that you can appreciate, and that your appreciation of it will be a function of your philosophy or theology or something else. If, on the other hand, I push *my* theory to the extreme, I find myself in as great a difficulty. I am quite aware of the ambiguity of the word 'understand'. In one sense, it means to understand without believing, for unless you can understand a view of life (let us say) without believing in it, the word 'understand' loses all meaning, and the act of choice between one view and another is reduced to caprice. But if you yourself are convinced of a certain view of life, then you irresistibly and inevitably believe that if anyone else comes to 'understand' it fully, his understanding *must* terminate in belief. . . . Actually one probably has more pleasure in the poetry when one shares the beliefs of the poet. On the other hand, there is a distinct pleasure in enjoying poetry as poetry when one does *not* share the beliefs, analogous to the pleasure of 'mastering' other men's philosophical systems." (*Selected Essays,* pp. 269–271.)

This theory of poetic assent is applicable not only to thought but also to feelings, and, without incurring the risk of being described as pure aestheticism or art for art's sake, it is bound to be valid for everyone except the few who look upon the arts as propaganda to be controlled by the state for political ends. Without sharing the hedonism of Omar Khayyam or the devout Catholicism of Dante, one can appreciate the music and dream-like quality of the former, and the sublime and terrifying beauty of the latter. "The poet who 'thinks' is merely the poet who can express the emotional equivalent of thought", Eliot has written; and he adds: "I can see no reason for believing that either Dante or Shakespeare did any thinking on his own." (*Selected Prose,* Penguin, 1953, pp. 53-54.) Yeats believed that the poet must know all philosophy but only admit it in his work on his own terms.

Eliot was, with Coleridge and Valéry, one of the rare poets

who could also think, and he devoted much time to the thought of philosophers—Eastern and Western—and above all to F. H. Bradley, whom he undertook to study as a subject for his doctoral thesis at Harvard, at the suggestion of his professor, Josiah Royce. The philosophical ideas of F.H. Bradley were in the air. They were a continuation and development from Platonic, Hegelian and Kantian ideas which had wide currency on the Continent, and they were consciously or subconsciously applied by Mallarmé and other writers, and by painters. The impressionist painters (Monet more than any other) were, like Bergson, much concerned with time, with the attempt to immobilize the fugitive sensation, to fix the instability of the passing moment and the flux of the ever-changing, thinking subject. Proust was concerned with the same quest. True artists and thinkers, like Bradley or Bergson, were all aware that they were living at the end of an age which was about to disappear and which they could not hold back. Kant had already discussed the difference between the noumenon and the phenomenon, and the impossibility of reaching the former, and Hegel, following Descartes, who had used God as the final mediator of truth, used the absolute instead. For Bradley, the ultimate subject of judgment is also the absolute, and the judging subject is a mode of the absolute, self-contradictory if taken to be independently actual. The judging subject has only an actualized duration, which is the expression of its relationship with the absolute, and a judgment is therefore an operation by which the absolute, through an actualized individuation, becomes temporarily conscious of itself. This is not only true Hegelianism, but it also connects with Bergson's notion of duration, as we shall see later.

Eliot in his essay on Bradley says: "The unity of Bradley's thought is not the unity attained by a man who never changes his mind. If he had so little occasion to change it, that is because he usually saw his problems from the beginning in all their complexity and connexions—saw them, in other words, with wisdom—and because he could never be deceived by his own metaphors—which, indeed, he used most sparingly—and was never tempted to make use of current nostrums. If all of

Bradley's writings are in some sense merely 'essays', that is not solely a matter of modesty, or caution, and certainly not of indifference, or even of ill health. It is that he perceived the contiguity and continuity of the various provinces of thought." (*Selected Essays*, pp. 415–416.) This assessment of Bradley explains some of Eliot's most fundamental attitudes, which were neither affectations nor poses, but the results of seriously held beliefs. He always argued that the meaning of a poem was variable according to the reader, and his approach to poetic or critical writing was always fluid and changing according to his beliefs. He changed his views on Milton, Shelley, Yeats, Goethe, Byron and many others, not because of any pressures, but as a normal development of his personality. He believed, as I do, that only mad people have "idées fixes". Bradley's scepticism and his notion of the fluidity of the personality, or of the ego, were part of the dominant notions of the age. So were the notion of the inextricability of the subject-object relationship, the notion that what we know of the past is our present experience of the past, and the notion that the author of the sonnets is not quite the same man as the author of *Hamlet*. As Eliot said, we die with the dying, we continuously change:

> The knowledge imposes a pattern, and falsifies,
> For the pattern is new in every moment
> And every moment is a new and shocking
> Valuation of all we have been.
> (*Four Quartets*, Faber, 1946, p. 18.)

We are part of an ever-moving Heraclitean flux, and objects and persons are always the immediate experience we have of them, and nothing more, for they quickly change. The person who boarded a train in a station is not the same person who alights at another station, and a person is the sum of these continuously changing experiences, while a poem is a duration, not only different for every reader, but also ever different in the life of the same reader. We are not quite in the Berkeleyan world in which things only are what the human existent makes them, but we are in a world, post-Kantian certainly, where a thing is the experience we have of it, and what the thing truly is we cannot know. We can see that the modern apostles of the impossibility of the communication of the true self of a person have invented nothing. The physical world is appearance, phenomenon, what one likes, and the mind knows intellectual coordination of these appearances, and, of course, is itself part of this world of appearances. This is in perfect conformity with Kantian mental categories, and with the precepts of cubism, which constructs mental representations of appearances, in an ever-moving, ever-changing, pure phenomenality. The poem is a duration which the reader apprehends, according to the scope and emphasis of his changing perceptions, and the dead writer's work being that which we know, our knowledge is therefore constantly changing and adjustable to the changes of the present. Shakespeare, placed in a landscape in which Milton and Dryden had not yet made their appearance, is bound to be different from Shakespeare looked at from the twentieth century, through the unavoidable prism of past ages which necessarily modify the vision we have of him. The past is therefore always changing and always influencing and transforming the present. Man is, as Locke or Kant would have put it, a perceiving animal, and he arranges his perceptions according to his beliefs and his inner mental and affective structures. We all try to find reasons for what we believe, and that includes scientists, who operate not in a vacuum but as continuously changing selves, surrounded by other, similarly changing, interacting selves. Neither the philosopher nor the poet ever starts the search for truth from axioms; they both start from a belief, a desire, an emotion or an urge to find the way of thinking or of expressing a glimpsed at or haunting truth, in a form which is mentally or aesthetically coherent and harmoniously integrated in as perfect a whole as possible. Scientists follow a similar path; they start, not from facts, but from hypotheses, which they endeavour to verify in all their various aspects and relationships. Starting from facts can only lead to statistical observations, but never to general principles.

Having briefly sketched the background or climate of the time in which Eliot began to write, and bearing in mind his profound dislike of biographical details, I should now merely confine

myself to the spirit of the advice which he himself puts at the
end of *A Choice of Kipling's Verse*:

> If I have given you delight
> By aught that I have done
> Let me lie quiet in that night
> Which shall be yours anon:
> And for the little, little span
> The dead are borne in mind,
> Seek not to question other than
> The books I leave behind.

This is the way he would have wished things to be, and this
is the way they will be, with the exception of a very brief
personal note, in order to try to dispose of two cruel and very
unjust remarks which have been made about his character.
They concern the question of his alleged anti-semitism and
that of his alleged pro-Fascist tendencies.

The first criticism rests, above all, on three lines of *Gerontion*, one of his rightly most famous poems, which is a masterpiece:

> And the jew squats on the window-sill, the owner,
> Spawned in some estaminet of Antwerp,
> Blistered in Brussels, patched and peeled in London.

The whole poem is a musical, complex and richly ambiguous
construction in which no suggestion, hint or image could or
should be looked upon as a mathematically verifiable statement. To do so is automatically to distort, for all the component elements of the poem hold together, as part of a whole,
and they can neither be used as demonstrations of the author's
opinions nor as isolated truths. It is obvious that no proprietor,
Jew or otherwise, spends his time sitting on his tenant's
window-sill. Such ubiquitousness in presence implies, in fact,
something more supernatural than a watchful Jew. It could
very well be Christ the Tiger. Anyway, the Jew as property
owner is merely a stock image. What matters is not the truth
of one single element, which could even be untrue in itself, or a
mere illusion, but the congruence of the elements to the whole
picture which contains good and bad and all sorts of aspects

of the life of an old man on the threshold of death. The syne-
doche is a figure of speech, but not a criterion of aesthetic
truth. Neither can one accommodate or transform everything
to suit contemporary attitudes and tastes. If we do so, we
merely deal in illusions; we either take the part for the whole,
or we do as Stalin did, we re-write history to suit our present
purpose and views. Thus, Ivan the Terrible can be, at will, a
tyrant or an archetypal hero. Eliot wrote this poem, and
*Burbank*, at the end of the First World War, and if one were
going to involve him retrospectively in the suffering of the Jews
which occurred twenty years later, then one might as well
involve Shakespeare and anyone who, in fun or in earnest,
made some unflattering remark about the Jews, including, of
course, those countries which, like Spain, on the one hand
rejected them, and on the other allowed them to hold some
of the highest posts in the land.

*Burbank with a Baedeker* is a mock-heroic description of
the life of the idle rich who haunt the dilapidated palaces of
Venice or other famous tourist centres, and lays no claim to
being taken seriously. It is written in the rumbustious style of
which young Eliot had already shown his mastery when he was
still at Harvard, when he wrote his merry fable about glutton
friars whom he wishes no more to malign than money-making
or money-lending Jews. He merely uses well-tried stock responses, and the lines:

> The rats are underneath the piles.
> The Jew is underneath the lot.

mean to me no more than that the rats are eating up the
rotting foundations of Venice, and money, represented in this
case by the Jew, is rotting or threatening the downfall of the
world. There is no ground for giving a literal meaning to what
is a construct-image in a picture. We all deal, alas, in stock
responses and in cliché phrases; the Jews have a reputation for
intelligence and genius in many domains, including money-
making, and those who are deficient in these qualities have
always been envious, and at times uncharitable enough to blame
them for it. As they are a very distinctive people, it is easy to

single out what look like defects and to play upon them, in the same way as, to give an example with which I am familiar, the French press never fails to call an evil-doer a Corsican if he is one, but if a Corsican happens to be a great poet like Valéry, then he is purely and simply a Frenchman.

Much as I dislike personal references, and I know that Eliot disliked them just as much, I feel I owe it to his memory to say that, having known him and continuously and regularly seen him for the last twenty-five years of his life, and being on the most affectionate terms, talking with absolutely full confidence on all kinds of subjects, I never heard him once make an uncharitable remark about Jews—or indeed about anyone else. He was too profoundly Christian, too imbued with the need for human brotherhood, too genuinely kind, to be disparaging about anyone. He always treated all human beings as equals, whatever their positions.

As for his so-called pro-Fascist tendencies, I shall simply quote a few words from a mutual friend, Herbert Read: "In all the years I knew him I never heard him express any sympathy for either Mussolini or Hitler—from his point of view they were godless men. 'The fundamental objection to fascist doctrine', he once wrote, 'the one that we conceal from ourselves because it might condemn ourselves, is that it is pagan.' He did not believe in democracy, and who can blame him? He believed in 'a community of Christians', and when it came to a close discussion of what he meant by this ideal, it seemed to have more in common with my anarchism than with any form of autocracy." (*T. S. Eliot, the Man and his Work*, edited by Allen Tate, Chatto & Windus, 1956, p. 30.) To these remarks I should add that he detested Nazism and Fascism as totally inhuman political systems. He believed in order, and in hierarchized society, but he above all believed that all men are equal in the eyes of God, and I have never known a man who could be so constantly and unfailingly kind, considerate for other people's views and merits, and ready to do anything to help people in need.

35

## II

## FROM *PRUFROCK AND OTHER OBSERVATIONS* TO *POEMS 1920*

In September 1914, Eliot met Pound, to whom he showed *Prufrock*. Pound declared it to be the best poem he had yet seen by an American, and after some efforts he succeeded in getting it published in June 1915 in *Poetry*, a magazine of verse edited by Harriet Monroe. In June 1917, *Prufrock and Other Observations* was published in volume form by *The Egoist*. What was the novelty of this slim volume of poems? In the famous essay, *Tradition and the Individual Talent*, which he wrote a little later in 1919, Eliot explained that: "The historical sense, which we may call nearly indispensable to anyone who would continue to be a poet beyond his twenty-fifth year . . . involves a perception, not only of the pastness of the past, but of its presence; the historical sense compels a man to write not merely with his own generation in his bones, but with a feeling that the whole of the literature of Europe from Homer and within it the whole of the literature of his own country has a simultaneous existence and composes a simultaneous order." (*Selected Essays*, p. 14.) And later in the same essay he said: "For my meaning is, that the poet has, not a 'personality' to express, but a particular medium, which is only a medium and not a personality, in which impressions and experiences combine in peculiar and unexpected ways." (*Idem*, pp. 19–20.) And later still: "Poetry is not a turning loose of emotion, but an escape from emotion; it is not the expression of personality, but an escape from personality. But, of course, only those who have personality and emotions know what it means to want to escape from these things." (*Idem*, p. 21.)

These few sentences extracted from a masterly essay con-

36

stitute a summary of what could be called Eliot's "art poétique". His Penelope, as Pound said about himself, was Flaubert, and his affinities were with the Symbolists, and naturally with Paul Valéry who, in *Le Cimetière Marin* and *La Jeune Parque*, applied principles similar to those he himself used. Eliot knew perfectly the mind of Europe, and this mind was not, at that moment, in tune with the mind which produced Georgian poetry, or with the "new frontiers spirit" of America. The poeticality of the Georgians, their journalistic desire to reach a wide public, repelled him. He did not want to write for a large public; he wanted to express the truth as he felt it, and those who wished to apprehend it would have to make the necessary effort. Above all, like Wordsworth or Donne, he wanted to move away from the poetical to ordinary language. Donne, tired of euphuism, had turned to colloquial, living speech; in the same way. Wordsworth, tired of artificial poeticalities, had wanted to return to natural, ordinary language, and to a poetry which, as Eliot put it, would have the strength and raciness of good prose, for a living language is made up of the speech rhythms of everyday life. With a consciousness and a sense of control which were very much attuned to the French poetic tradition, Eliot set about his task with deliberation, and he applied these principles in his poems as well as in his plays. He did whatever he did, ever conscious of his responsibilities to the past, to the language which he was using, and to the tradition which he was upholding, and he always endeavoured to achieve a mastery of expression and a transparency of language which effortlessly embody the progressive growth of his experience, which extends from *Prufrock* to the *Quartets*, and is also that of his age.

*The Love Song of J. Alfred Prufrock* is a monologue either by its author or by this imaginary character called Prufrock. Who knows? The title is as enticing as Coleridge's famous first line: "In Xanadu did Kubla Khan. . . ." The love song of a most mysterious, strangely indefinable person! From the start the reader is taken out of reality and launched into a world of dreams, on the wings of an internal monologue which is not meant to be overheard, and therefore not to be apprehended logically. The epigraph from Dante suggests just that: "If I believed that I spoke to a person who might go back alive to the world, this flame would shake no more. But since no one goes back alive out of this abyss (if what I hear is true), without fear of infamy I speak to you." Comforted by this thought, the speaker, whoever he may be, begins, as abruptly and colloquially as is the case with many poems of Donne:

> Let us go then, you and I,
> When the evening is spread out against the sky
> Like a patient etherised upon a table. . . .

The images are sharply defined, clearcut and transferable; obviously it is not only the evening which is a patient etherized upon a table but also the speaker, who is in a kind of inferno-like situation, in which he walks along muttering streets and summons up memories of grey nights in cheap hotels. And where is he going? To a given place? He does not know, but he remembers, at that very moment, a scene with light-headed cocktail women coming and going, and talking of Michelangelo. The drum roll of the last words, the music of the lines, are masterly, and compare farourably with the best of Tennyson. The description of this inferno-like scene continues in a more personal way, yet without separating the one who experiences from the experience. The fog is all round, including, of course, the soul of the speaker, who moves about with it. But what is the point of all this, where are "they" going? What question could be asked? The speaker immediately brushes the notion of an answer aside, by saying: "There will be time", time for all sorts of inanities, time for waiters or hostesses, or anyone, to drop questions on his plate, time to create—though that is doubtful; time to murder, or to destroy, and that is more likely; and time for indecisions and revisions, "before the taking of a toast and tea".

There is always time, but will the speaker dare to take a decision; will he dare to turn back? He suddenly becomes extremely self-conscious about all sorts of aspects of himself. He imagines someone looking at him from above, and noticing his bald pate and his thin legs; and he asks himself: is all this trouble worth it, is it worth disturbing the universe for futilities?

> Do I dare
> Disturb the universe?
> In a minute there is time
> For decisions and revisions which a minute will reverse.

The way up and the way down are the same, as Heraclitus put it, and one minute undoes what another has done, so why do anything? "For I have known them all already, known them all." "La vie est courte, hélas, et j'ai lu tous les livres", said Mallarmé. Prufrock's life is all in the past, without future, hence his constant feeling that he is old. Having "known them all", and knowing so much, what is the use of doing anything? And of course the question is: what kind of truth has the speaker known?—merely the vacuity and futility of life, summed up in the lines:

> I have measured out my life with coffee spoons. . . .
> And I have known the eyes already, known them all.

Eyes, smells and stairs play a very important role in Eliot's poetry. Stairs always imply abasement, suffering and effort in order to achieve something. And true enough, the speaker has no sooner mounted half or so of the stairs, to meet we don't know whom, perhaps to pop some question, or take tea with someone, than he wonders if he should not turn back. The eyes are the consciousness of the human being, and they can "formulate you, sprawling on a pin". In the end, what can one do?—since, as he says:

> . . . I have known the arms already, known them all—
> Arms that are braceleted and white and bare
> (But in the lamplight, downed with light brown hair!)

Perhaps he is thinking of Donne's "bracelet of bright hair about the bone", yet he wonders, being as susceptible to perfume as Baudelaire:

> Is it perfume from a dress
> That makes me so digress?

And with that he is back to his indecisions and his dreams of the popular quarters of towns. He soon realizes his inadaptation to urban life, and how much better he could have been if he had lived in some dream world, or if he had been, not even an animal, like a crab, but only part of one—a pair of ragged claws. The day passes; we are back to the evening, and once more to the question: "What should I do?" The same question which the young man carbuncular of *The Waste Land* asks himself comes to his mind:

> Should I, after tea and cakes and ices,
> Have the strength to force the moment to its crisis?

But how could he? He is so inhibited, he has "seen his head (grown slightly bald) brought in upon a platter" like that of St. John the Baptist—a great prophet. He certainly is no prophet, so how could he presume as to what might happen? Anyway, it does not matter; he will go away as usual, accompanied by the sniggers of the eternal Footman. And after all, would it have been worth while, amid such trivialities, "to have squeezed the universe into a ball", as Marvell proposed to do with his "Coy Mistress", or "to say: 'I am Lazarus, come from the dead' ", full of wisdom, having had a glimpse of the great mystery? Alas, he is neither a prophet nor a great sage; he is merely a perplexed, unheroic, inhibited, twentieth-century young man. The argument starts again, and the question is once more raised: should he have dared? And again the same answer: "Would it have been worth while?"—for the lady, turning towards the window, could say:

> 'That is not it at all,
> That is not what I meant, at all.'

All these hesitations and indecisions bring forth the image of Hamlet, the archetype of hesitation, but the speaker hastens to say: "No! I am not Prince Hamlet, nor was meant to be." "Prince" is the important word; there is no doubt something Hamletian in his hesitations, but absolutely nothing heroic in him; no, he is merely an attendant, a man of no great importance, a tool—"Almost, at times, the Fool". And that notion brings him back to earth and to his obsession with age: "I grow old . . . I grow old . . .", which he punctures by the clownish remark: "I shall wear the bottoms of my trousers rolled." This is followed by the comic picture of thin wisps of hair parted and glued on the back of the head, and by the bold suggestion of eating a peach, whatever such a gesture may imply. After that, he will walk on the beach, where he once heard the mermaids sing each to each, though not to him; and that plunges him into visions of the chambers of the sea of *The Tempest*, or of Ulysses' voyages to Circe's island, with sea nymphs wreathed with seaweeds, until human voices awaken him from this delightful dream. Then, instead of accepting truly to live, he throws himself into elements in which he will have no thinking to do; he will only have to let himself go, and mermaids will perhaps bring him the peace of facile pleasures.

*Portrait of a Lady*, which Eliot wrote at about the same time as *Prufrock*, did not please Pound to the same extent. In fact, he even tried to discourage Eliot from publishing these two poems together in *Poetry*, though he published it, later in the same year, in an anthology edited by himself. The music of the verse is not as sustainedly beautiful as that of *Prufrock*. The form is also different; this is not a dramatic monologue, but an imaginary conversation between two real people. The lady is admirably portrayed, and she is the forerunner of a category of ladies of whom Eliot made masterly use in *The Waste Land*, *The Cocktail Party*, *The Confidential Clerk* and *The Elder Statesman*. Eliot's observations and descriptions of this person are those of a born dramatist who can single out and stress the exact detail or gesture in order to express character.

Smoke and fog continue to be the two attributes of urban life, and the poem begins again, like *Prufrock*, in the smoke and fog of a December night, in a drawing-room which has "an atmosphere of Juliet's tomb". The ritualistic inanities of modern life begin to unfold: music, the weather, social gossip and snobbery, suggested by the thought that Chopin's soul should be resurrected for only two or three select people. After this prelude come the confidences and advances, slowly proceeding or halting, according to the modulations of the verse, producing such a perfect blend of content and form that it makes the talking lady leap fully alive from the page:

'You do not know how much they mean to me, my friends,
And how, how rare and strange it is, to find
In a life composed so much, so much of odds and ends,
(For indeed I do not love it . . . you knew? you are not blind!

How keen you are!)
To find a friend who has these qualities,
Who has, and gives
Those qualities upon which friendship lives.'

This is both precise and pressing in its demands for a response, something which throws the visitor into confusion, and into a state of acute self-consciousness from which he tries to escape with a certain amount of forced ease, suggested by the fact that we not only have Chopin's piano music, but also violins and cornets and a dull tom-tom, producing in fact a cacophony that obviously suggests a violent headache, which he tries to mitigate with the words:

—Let us take the air, in a tobacco trance,
Admire the monuments,
Discuss the late events. . . .

Time passes, the lilacs are in bloom; "she has a bowl of lilacs in her room", and she pursues her dreams, thoughtlessly twisting and breaking the lilac stalks which she holds in her hands:
" 'Ah, my friend, you do not know, you do not know. . . .' "
He smiles and goes on drinking tea. She dreams of the fleetingness of life, and he goes on drinking tea, while she prattles on:

'I am always sure that you understand
My feelings, always sure that you feel,
Sure that across the gulf you reach your hand.'

Then she switches to a plangent tone, which only enhances his callousness and his indifference:

'But what have I, but what have I, my friend,
To give you, what can you receive from me?'

42

No reply. So she ends with the words:

> 'I shall sit here, serving tea to friends. . . .'
> I take my hat: how can I make a cowardly amends
> For what she has said to me?

He does not, he remains self-possessed, like Prufrock, even in spite of the scent of hyacinths fleeting across the garden.

In October he has made up his mind to tell her of his decision to go abroad; so he mounts the stairs, the famous stairs, which in Eliot's poetry indicate effort, tension, slow progression, towards a decision made or still to be made. Here the climbing of the stairs is literal and painful: "And feel as if I had mounted on my hands and knees." He confesses his desire to leave:

> 'And so you are going abroad; and when do you return? . . .'
> My smile falls heavily among the bric-à-brac.

—that is to say, over the world that he has shattered to pieces. "'Perhaps you can write to me.'" He does not answer, and so she goes on:

> 'For everybody said so, all our friends,
> They all were sure our feelings would relate
> So closely! I myself can hardly understand.
> We must leave it now to fate.
> You will write, at any rate.
> Perhaps it is not too late.
> I shall sit here, serving tea to friends.'

We are again back to tea, and to the waste of time. The young man keeps his imperturbable control as usual: "Let us take the air, in a tobacco trance—" Yet at last one doubt creeps upon him: what if, after all this begging and imploring unanswered, she should die? "Would she not have the advantage, after all?" This is followed by a pirouette about the "dying fall" of music, and a question which is left purposedly unanswered: "And should I have the right to smile?"

The poems which compose the rest of the volume entitled *Prufrock and Other Observations* all bear the mark of the same atmosphere of aimlessness and of the futility of life, whether apprehended personally or looked at from the outside. The fog, the haunting hours of dusk, are Dantesque; the ironies and twists of responses, the reminiscences of mnemonic rhythms and attitudes echo Laforgue, Corbière, Verlaine and Gautier. The sense of boredom and of squalor, the viscosity of the past from which the present cannot escape, and the limbo world in which nothing has any value and nothing is truly done, connect with both Dante and Baudelaire. The allusiveness, the suggestiveness, the careful juxtaposition of contrasted images, the swift changes of mood, the sharp confrontations of past and present, of the commonplace and the horrible, with the singing of mermaids or with the desire to escape to sea floors or sea caves, the various symbols used in order to convey certain emotions or attitudes, constitute the innovations which Eliot brought to poetry.

The four *Preludes*, written at different times, suggest at least two slightly different phases which coincide with the moments at which they were written. The first two *Preludes* were written at Harvard, in 1909–1910, just before *Conversations Galantes*. They could, whether it is intentional or not, be described as imagist, in the sense that the images do all the work, without any anthropomorphic suggestion, as if these images had come together by themselves in order to form a picture of desolate urban life:

> The winter evening settles down
> With smell of steaks in passageways.
> Six o'clock.
> The burnt-out ends of smoky days.

The second *Prelude* exhibits the same characteristics. The third and fourth, written a year later in Paris, are different in the sense that they are held together by an imaginary witness. The climate is Baudelairian; the soul is a marsh in which float sordid creatures, and the vision of the person sitting on the edge of the bed:

> You curled the papers from your hair,
> Or clasped the yellow soles of feet
> In the palms of both soiled hands

is that of a realistic painting. The last *Prelude* reinforces the atmosphere of widespread desolation and hopelessness in which one can sense

> The conscience of a blackened street
> Impatient to assume the world.

And the witness of this scene can bear no more, and dreams of

> some infinitely gentle
> Infinitely suffering thing

—which could only be a redeeming figure like that of Christ or the Holy Virgin. After a sudden revolt against this passing weakness, a resolution is taken:

> Wipe your hand across your mouth, and laugh;
> The worlds revolve like ancient women
> Gathering fuel in vacant lots.

The world without faith is as empty as the world of the women of Canterbury, who suffer and bemoan the absence of their beloved archbishop.

*Rhapsody on a Windy Night,* written in Paris, continues the merciless exposure of the shallowness and sordidness of town life in cadences reminiscent of Verlaine and Laforgue, but also with some striking and practically archetypal images which are already an integral part of Eliot's poetry:

> Midnight shakes the memory
> As a madman shakes a dead geranium.

A door opens "like a grin", a cat "slips out its tongue and devours a morsel of rancid butter". Without the slightest comment, just as if it were a camera objectively recording what happens, the poet places side by side with this image the picture of a child whose hand, like the cat's tongue, "automatic, slipped out and pocketed a toy that was running along the quay". "The memory throws up high and dry a crowd of twisted things"; it is very much like the sea in *Dry Salvages.* Finally, the wanderer in the night, the speaker of the poem, has to mount stairs to his Calvary, his bed, so as to sleep and to prepare for life—"The last twist of the knife". Memory is only a store of sordid fragments, thrown up into consciousness helter-skelter, according to the rhythm of the emotions which summon them. The future does not exist, the present is unbearable, and the past, as in Baudelaire, is both unshakeable and unredeemable. So, as Baudelaire said in his *Journal Intime*: "What, in Heaven's name, has this world henceforth to do? . . . Progress has atrophied in us all that is spiritual . . . and there cannot be any progress (true progress, that is to say moral progress) except within the individual himself." There only remains to do as Baudelaire did, to cultivate "hysteria with delight and horror," the "dereglement des sens" of Rimbaud, or suicide.

The reader of the *Boston Evening Transcript* has also to mount the steps and to ring the bell, "turning wearily, as one would turn to nod good-bye to Rochefoucauld", the great exponent of men's incorrigible and inherent egoism.

Last, but not least, the famous *La Figlia Che Piange*. She stands on the highest pavement of the stairs, not for a difficult access, but for a difficult, painful parting. She weaves the sunlight in her hair; the sunlight, or a shaft of sunlight, is for Eliot always synonymous with inspiration and happiness. She clasps a bunch of flowers in her arms, composing the perfect picture of a dream which was unfulfilled and which troubled the poet's midnight and noon's repose. The actual Figlia Che Piange is supposed to have been a statue in a museum in the North of Italy, which the poet failed to find in the course of one of his visits to that part of the world. Yet he always remembered the image of this statue. Whatever the starting-point of this beautiful poem, it is above all the picture of the idyllic unfulfilled dream of the love of two people, so well attuned to each other that they would have met and parted in "some way incomparably light and deft, . . . simple and faithless as a smile and shake of the hand", as Gautier had put it. Coming at the close of a period of greyness, this beautiful lyric, one of the most graceful, haunting pictures of dream happiness which Eliot ever suggested, is like a shaft of sunlight on a November day.

*Gerontion*, written in 1919 and published in *Poems 1920*, is supposed to have been one of the sections of *The Waste*

*Land*, which Pound's surgical hand cut out and condemned to go by itself. If it is, he was certainly right, for *Gerontion* is a perfectly self-contained, perfectly orchestrated and structured whole, and is one of the best and most moving poems that Eliot ever wrote. It seems impossible to make an adequate place for it in *The Waste Land*; that is why, although it was written at the time of *The Waste Land* and therefore partakes of its mood, it is difficult to believe that Eliot ever meant it to be part of it. It is composed in a form of which Eliot was already a master, the symphonic form, which he used so successfully in *The Waste Land* and the *Quartets*. It is therefore difficult to see how this symphonic poem could be part of a larger symphony, for just as Mallarmé replied to Debussy, when asked by him if he could put *L'Après-Midi d'un Faune* to music, "I thought I had already done so myself", Eliot could give the same answer to any composer who put to him a similar question. This poem is music, and together with Mallarmé, Valéry and Verlaine, Eliot fully participates in the poets' task which consists in "reprendre à la musique leur bien".

If *Prufrock* is the tragi-comedy of a serious quest for truth, by a person who ends in falling back in the arms of the mermaids with whom he has already played or whom he has already used as opium to relieve his ennui, *Gerontion* is a tragedy. After his quests and his failures, his knowledge of himself and of the world, and as he has long since purged his self of the Baudelairian and Prufrockian notion of trying to find the necessary courage "de contempler mon coeur et mon corps sans dégoût", he can only wait for death, which cannot be far off. The poem begins with the same dramatic, button-holing excitement as *Prufrock*: "Here I am, an old man in a dry month." What a striking picture! One can at once see this waif-like creature with lips and skin parched up by the sun and the years, standing in the crackling light of July or August, a creature who cannot even read, who has to be read to by a boy, and who is waiting for rain, the kind of rain which will only come after *The Waste Land*. Yet, in spite of his apparent weakness, he proceeds to describe, with great vigour and unforgettable precision of style, his situation and his surroundings. He "was neither at the hot gates", whatever they may be—perhaps the gates of the Western front, or the Thermopylae—nor did he ever fight in colonial wars, heaving a cutlass, "bitten by flies, fought". This last word stands alone, reverberating back on the whole preceding passage the stubborn vigour of this old man. After this, he proceeds with the description of his house and of his landlord, whoever he may be. The house is decayed, like himself, like the civilization to which he belongs. The landlord is a Jew, "spawned in some estaminet"—a word reminiscent of the 1914–1918 war, and also, of course, of another inn, where another Jew was born 2,000 years ago. Anyway, this Jewish landlord is truly, like all Jews, cosmopolitan; Antwerp, Brussels, London are the towns where he has lived. But there again, so was in fact the other, long-shadowed Jew, Christ, whose presence will soon be felt. Talking about Him, the towns to mention would be Bethlehem, Jerusalem, Rome, the world! As was suggested in the previous chapter, where this poem was briefly discussed, landlords do not sit on the window-sills of their tenants' houses, and the lines:

> The goat coughs at night in the field overhead;
> Rocks, moss, stonecrop, iron, merds

indicate above all a stony, Mediterranean landscape, where the goat, from the Greeks to our times, is still the most precious of domestic animals. We are certainly not in the lush meadows of Holland. This comment is simply meant to indicate that the literal meaning of the words here, or in any modern poem, is not what matters. The Jew, whoever he is, is undefinable. The woman who looks after Gerontion, or is some kind of companion to him, is in no better state than he is. After this descriptive passage, there is a pause in order to sum up or to restate the most important point or truth which emanates from it:

> I an old man,
> A dull head among windy spaces.

This breath-taking, wide-ranging, perfectly orchestrated phrase marks the end of the first movement. After that, anything could emerge from these windy spaces. Full of expectancy, we raise our eyes, like Marlowe's Dr. Faustus, waiting for a sign, and the word "signs" begins, in fact, the second movement:

> Signs are taken for wonders. 'We would see a sign!'
> The word within a word. . . .

—that is to say, Christ; and Christ cannot be far away:

> In the juvescence of the year
> Came Christ the tiger.

"Juvescence" is a bold neologism, necessary to the prosody, which could not stand another syllable, yet it is also the right and necessary word, the word which indicates the sprouting and growing youth of the world—Spring. As in *The Waste Land*, Spring or April is a cruel time, and Christ comes not as a healer or redeemer, for in order that it might be so, one has to deserve Him, but as a tiger; and we do not know, or we are not told what this tiger will do. April, in Eliot's poems, the month of Christ's coming, the month of Chaucerian pilgrimages, is followed by depraved, luscious May, overflowing with fruit "to be eaten, to be divided, to be drunk", so as to forget the terror of the tiger, through the pleasures of the senses, in the shadow of the flowering judas—and Judas is also the name of the betrayer of Christ. The words "to be eaten, to be divided, to be drunk among whispers" could, of course, both apply to the body of Christ divided up amidst religious whispers, as well as to earthly fruits and profits divided up amidst conspiratorial whispers. The flurry of foreign names which follows is simply meant to suggest cosmopolitan finance and corruption. So we have Mr. Silvero, with silver in his name, Madame de Tornquist, a very taunting name, difficult to find anywhere else except in an Eliotian list of names, Fraülein von Kulp, or Von Culpa, as guilty as anyone, who stood with her hand on the door. Which door? Gerontion, windy head, cannot remember. Anyway, it does not matter. All these people are merely part of a gyrating, whirling humanity, producing nothing: "Vacant shuttles weave the wind." What a magnifi-

49

cent image! One may weave the wind or the waves, but nothing will come out of nothing, not even ghosts: "I have no ghosts", says Gerontion, no memories:

> An old man in a draughty house
> Under a windy knob.

This is the end of the second movement. He is again on the edge of the universe. Anything can happen, and he himself starts the meditation and asks the question: "After such knowledge, what forgiveness?" But the question is: What kind of knowledge is he alluding to? Is it the knowledge of long and numerous experiences? To whom is Gerontion speaking? With whom is he pleading for his behaviour? In all probability with Christ, whom he later offers to meet honestly, but first he must explain the causes of his various failures. History, personalized history, more feminine than masculine, can, as he says, deceive with whispering ambitions or beguile with vanities; she gives when one is not ready to receive, and she gives with supple confusions, confusions which, since they are "supple", are in fact wiles to incite our desires, in the same way as Cleopatra's giving merely famished the desires of the receiver; or she gives too late, or too soon, when one is not prepared for it, and therefore one dispenses with history. "Neither fear nor courage saves us." Heroism sometimes fathers vices, and sometimes virtues are born from our crimes. Tears of regret are shaken in vain "from the wrath-bearing tree": that is, of course, the tree of life, which can produce only tears and suffering.

The fourth movement begins with:

> The tiger springs in the new year. Us he devours. . . .

But, says Gerontion, "we have not reached conclusion". "We" refers to the speaker and to his interlocutor; "conclusion" means both agreement and end; and the speaker, the "I", is stiff with age, therefore half-dead, in a ruined house, living, like all men, in a rented house or inn, in a world which he does not control. Yet, the speaker says, I do not make these confessions on purpose, or under the terror or on the advice of devils. Then comes a conciliatory move towards Christ: "I would meet you upon this honestly." I lost my faith, I lost therefore beauty in terror, and terror in questioning; I have lost all passion, and what is the use of keeping any, since whatever I could keep is tainted, adulterated; and this is followed by the plangent cry contained in the last lines: "I have lost my sight, smell, hearing, taste and touch"; I have therefore lost the use of all my senses, so "how should I use them for your closer contact?"

After that comes the finale of the poem, which is a splendid piece of rich, complex ambiguities opening up on wide horizons, to close suddenly and dramatically with the stark, concrete image of the last two lines:

> Tenants of the house,
> Thoughts of a dry brain in a dry season.

The first five lines of this finale sum up the hopelessness and nastiness of Gerontion's life, and of his present situation. All these reminiscences and deliberations merely give the illusion of a chilled delirium, they merely excite the mind when the senses have cooled or are half-frozen, and therefore they only afford an impression of variety, which is merely illusion, reflected over and over again, as is suggested by the marvellous image, "a wilderness of mirrors". This does not prevent either the spider or the weevil from going on with their business of burrowing and killing. What happened to people like De Bailhache, Fresca, Mrs. Cammel, who are obviously a cosmopolitan lot, is a way of indicating that their fate involves the whole world. They are all dead, they are whirling atoms in the constellation of the Bear, no more important than a dead gull in the windy straits of Belle Isle or Cape Horn, leaving behind only a "white feather", which the abyss claims, and an old man, he too driven by the winds to a sleepy corner. All these thoughts have no reality; they are merely the tenants of a house, a decayed house, part of a barren world or a civilization about to crumble down into dust.

By 1917 Eliot began to worry, as he himself said, "that he might have dried up completely"; "I had not written anything for some time and I began to feel desperate." He tried to write in French and he discovered that he could do so. Pound apparently went through the poems which he wrote at that period, made a few notes concerning words and rhythms, and suggested the reading of Théophile Gautier's *Emaux et Camées*. "We studied Gautier and then we thought, 'Have I anything to say in which this form will be useful', and we experimented. The form gave the impetus to the content." (*Paris Review*, Spring/Summer 1959.) The first of the poems was *The Hippopotamus*. The French poems, *Sweeney* and *Whispers of Immortality*, were also much discussed with Pound, who says about the latter: "How . . . you can influence another chap's subject-matter, unless you actually write his . . . poems for him . . . I don't quite know. Only case where I tried it was a success. I led Eliot up to her wot *(sic)* posterity now knows as 'Grishkin' with the firm intuito that a poem wd. result & intention that it should. But that *is* an UNIQUE experiment in my annals." (Ezra Pound to H. B. P[arkes], 16 December [1931?]; photographic copy at the Academic Center Library, University of Texas, Austin, Texas.)

The influence of Pound on the career and development of Eliot as a poet cannot be underestimated. Pound not only helped him to publish his first poems in reviews and book form, but he also fought very hard to impose Eliot as a young poet of great promise, and as a writer who deserved all the help that he could get. Eliot, of course, had a great admiration for Pound. "Mr. Pound", said Eliot, "is probably the most important living poet in our language." (*After Strange Gods,* Faber, 1934, p. 42.) "Pound's great contribution to the work of other poets . . . is his insistence upon the immensity of the amount of *conscious* labor to be performed by the poet; and his invaluable suggestions for the kind of training the poet should give himself . . ." ("Ezra Pound" in *Poetry*, Chicago (September 1946), pp. 337–338.) Earlier in this same essay Eliot had said: "Pound . . . created a situation in which, for the first time . . . English and American poets collaborated, knew each other's works, and influenced each other. . . . If it had not been for the work that Pound did in the years [1910–22] . . . the isolation of American poetry, and the isolation of individual American poets, might have continued for a long time." (*Idem*, pp. 330–

331.) Pound had read widely—Italian, French, Provençal and Chinese poetry; he favoured precision in the use of contemporary speech, and he favoured the use of subject-matter and themes and images related to contemporary life. He was against the purely poetical which was fashionable in England at the beginning of the century. Yeats was then still struggling with his post-Romantic and pre-Raphaelite phase, and this is what he himself says: "I was unlike others of my generation, in one thing only. I am very religious, and deprived by Huxley and Tyndall, whom I detested, of the simple-minded religion of my childhood, I had made a new religion, almost an infallible church, of poetic tradition, of a fardel of stories and of personages and of emotions, inseparable from their first expression, passed on from generation to generation by poets and painters with some help from philosophers and theologians." (*The Trembling of the Veil*, quoted by T. S. Eliot in *After Strange Gods*, p. 44.)

Ezra Pound, who was for a time W. B. Yeats' secretary, "insisted that poetry was an art, an art which demanded the most arduous application and study, and he insisted in saying that in our time it had to be a highly conscious art"; he also said that "a poet who knows only the poetry of his own language is as poorly equipped as the painter or the musician who knows only the painting and music of his century." (Ezra Pound, *The New English Review*, November 1946.) T. S. Eliot, who shared these views, obviously derived comfort from this support, which came not only from Pound and from the whole Symbolist and post-Symbolist movement, but particularly from Mallarmé and from Valéry, whom he knew and admired. Consciousness, effort, and a certain disdain of popularity, or of wilfully writing for a popular audience, were the criteria which were prevalent in France at that moment, and which Eliot followed. Pound not only helped Eliot to publish *Prufrock*; he also reviewed it and praised it in *The Egoist* in 1917, and later in *The Little Review*, and, to crown his effort, he persuaded Alfred Knopf to publish *Poems* by T. S. Eliot in 1920.

The most striking of these poems is undoubtedly *Gerontion*, but to say so is not to say that the others lack distinction or interest. Far from it. The poems in French continue to depict the same grey type of desiccated, impersonal, barren, grotesque, hollow life which was the hallmark of the previous group of poems. The sordid scamperings of *Lune de Miel* in which a newly-wed couple hurtle along from city to city, seeing nothing, the admirable description of "le garçon délabré qui n'a rien à faire" in the poem *Dans le Restaurant*, are full of humour and irony. The latter poem ends with Phlebas, the Phoenician sailor, the symbol of peregrinations, who perishes under the water, an element which appears again and again in the poetry of Eliot, and which has various connotations and meanings. *Le Directeur, Mélange Adultère de Tout*—describing Eliot "à la Corbière", and the *Sweeney* poems, are full of savage humour. Still, in spite of the fascination which this kind of humour can exercise, the two most important and most striking poems of the group, excepting of course *Gerontion*, are *The Hippopotamus* and the memorable *Whispers of Immortality*. The "hippopotamus" is the church, broad-backed, resting on its belly in the mud, and merely flesh and blood, therefore capable of errors and misdirection:

> The hippo's feeble steps may err
> In compassing material ends,
> While the True Church need never stir
> To gather in its dividends.

These dividends come from everywhere, and the true church transcends all limitations, but when the hippo takes wings:

> He shall be washed as white as snow,
> By all the martyr'd virgins kist,
> While the True Church remains below
> Wrapt in the old miasmal mist.

*Whispers of Immortality* is replete with striking, contrasting images and aspects of life from different ages. We pass without transition from the age of Webster and Donne to that of Gautier and the atmosphere of nineteenth-century "fin de siècle". Carmen, with her dark eyes, becomes Grishkin, promising pneumatic bliss and sheer sensuality. *Whispers of Immortality* are

certainly not *Intimations of Immortality*; the two poems belong
to different ages.

> Webster was much possessed by death
> And saw the skull beneath the skin;
> . . .
> Donne, I suppose, was such another
> Who found no substitute for sense. . . .

But Donne and Webster knew, as Shakespeare or Marvell knew,
that:

> The grave's a fine and private place,
> But none, I think, do there embrace.

There is no possible contact with the flesh in order to allay the
fever of the bone. In the age of Donne, nothing could explain
or allay the thirst for the mystery or the inherent human longing for knowing the whole truth about life. The modern world
is different. Grishkin, uncorseted, will easily satisfy the need
of the sensual Brazilian jaguar,* without any waste of time
devoted to metaphysical speculations. With Grishkin, abstract
entities do not exist, or they are quickly dispelled by the
dominating presence of her body, and ours crawl between dry,
skeletal ribs, as between sheets to keep our metaphysics warm.
Grishkin thinks with her body, and her body's presence
abolishes all thoughts:

> And even the Abstract Entities
> Circumambulate her charm;
> But our lot crawls between dry ribs
> To keep our metaphysics warm.

---

* It is strange that in Balzac's *La Cousine Bette* there is a rich young
man from Brazil, who is enjoying the gay life of Paris and who is described as "the Brazilian jaguar".

## III

## *THE WASTE LAND* AND *THE HOLLOW MEN*

Pound's influence on Eliot's work is nowhere more telling than in the case of *The Waste Land*, which he annotated, pruned by half and reduced to the shape which it now has. The publication of the facsimile of the original manuscript makes clear Pound's contribution to this work. Eliot was at that time unwell, and therefore unable to detach himself from his work and to look at it critically. Had he allowed time to elapse so as to recover his health, he would have attended to his writing in an objective and controlled frame of mind and feelings, which would, I am sure, have enabled him to discover some, if not all, of the weaknesses which Pound spotted and disposed of. The fifty-four lines of naturalistic narration of brothel-life-cum-police-discussion in demotic English would have encumbered the main theme of the poem, at least as much as the long narrative of a shipwreck which was part of *Death by Water*. There is no doubt that Pound's critical acumen and the imaginative empathy, which enabled him to grasp the intricate workings of Eliot's genius and the range and depth of experience which he was endeavouring to express, are of a high order and extremely rare in literature. Wordsworth and Coleridge are the names which come to mind. Eliot was certainly pleased with Pound's help, and he said so explicitly, and dedicated *The Waste Land* to him with the words: "il miglior fabbro".

Eliot had apparently had *The Waste Land* in mind as early as 5th November 1919, when he said in a letter to Quinn: "I am now at work on an article ordered by *The Times*, and when that is off, I hope to get started on a poem I have in mind." (T. S. Eliot, *The Waste Land*, a facsimile and transcript, Faber, 1971, p. xviii.) On the 9th of May he confirmed to Quinn that the poem was partly on paper. From mid-October 1921, his enforced rest-cure gave him the necessary leisure for writing. It was probably at this stage of composition that he applied to the first two sections of his work as a tentative title the quotation from Dickens's *Our Mutual Friend*, "He Do the Police in Different Voices". The first manuscript was about twice the length of the poem as published, of which the central core seems to have been basically the five-part poem we have, but with three additional long passages, with nine miscellaneous poems of varying length from five to eighty-three lines—the latter being the length of a long passage which was the opening of *Death by Water*. This passage, inspired by the Ulysses canto (XXVI) of Dante's *Inferno*, and also influenced by Tennyson's *Ulysses*, was discarded by Pound.

The original opening of the poem was an account, in fifty-four lines, of a low-life evening in a town which could have been St. Louis, Boston, London or, more probably, Joyce's Dublin. As for the language used, Eliot had explained, in the *Chapbook* for April 1921, that ". . . verse is always struggling, while remaining verse, to take up to itself more and more of what is prose, to take something more from life and turn it into 'play'. . . . The real failure of the mass of contemporary verse is its failure to draw anything new from life into art." The ideal for the handling of this type of subject-matter was represented by the work of Marie Lloyd: ". . . whereas other comedians amuse their audiences as much and sometimes more than Marie Lloyd, no other comedian succeeded so well in giving expression to the life of that audience, in raising it to a kind of art. It was, I think, this capacity for expressing the soul of the people that made Marie Lloyd unique, and that made her audiences, even when they joined in the chorus, not so much hilarious as happy." (*Selected Essays*, p. 419.)

The original opening of Part III, about forty-five couplets in imitation of Pope's *Rape of the Lock*, was intended to introduce another voice and another rhythm, to raise into "play" the kind of upper-middle-class life described. "Pound", says Eliot, "induced me to destroy what I thought an excellent set of couplets; for, said he, 'Pope has done this so well that you cannot do it better; and if you mean this as a burlesque, you had better suppress it, for you cannot parody Pope unless you can write better verse than Pope—and you can't.' " (Introduction by T. S. Eliot to Ezra Pound's *Selected Poems*, Faber & Gwyer, 1928, p. xxi.)

Whatever one may think about the long passages which Pound persuaded Eliot to omit, there can be no question as to the contribution made, at that time, to the poem by most of his deletions. Two shorter passages, one of fifteen lines, an apostrophe to London, and one of eight lines about Highbury, were cancelled, and by dropping twenty lines he improved the long passage in Part III describing the mechanical sexual encounter between the "typist home at teatime" and "the young man carbuncular". Donald Gallup says that "having decided to accept all of Pound's important suggestions and many of the less significant ones, Eliot was relieved to be rid of the poem and free to turn his mind to the planning of the *Criterion*. (Six months later, probably in order that there should be no second thoughts about any of the deleted sections, he offered to give his only copies of them to John Quinn, and sent them off to New York on 23rd October 1922.) . . . In giving the original manuscript to John Quinn in 1922, Eliot explained that he considered it worth preserving in this form 'solely for the reason that it is the only evidence of the difference which [Pound's] . . . criticism has made to this poem', and in a later reference to it (in 1932) he stated that its principal value was 'As a masterpiece of critical literature'." (Henry W. Wenning, *T. S. Eliot and Ezra Pound*, C. A. Stonehill, Inc., New Haven, 1970, pp. 21–24.)

The writing of the notes was merely due to the fact that the poem was too short to be printed by itself in one volume, so Eliot decided to "spike the guns of critics of my earlier poems who had accused me of plagiarism. . . . I have sometimes thought of getting rid of these notes; but now they can never be unstuck. They have had almost greater popularity than the poem itself." (*On Poetry and Poets*, Faber, 1957, pp. 109–110.) In 1924 Pound said: ". . . I did not see the notes till six or eight months afterwards; and they have not increased my enjoyment of the poem one atom. The poem seems to me an emotional unit. . . . I have not read Miss Weston's *Ritual to Romance*, and do not at present intend to. As to the citations, I do not think it matters a damn which is from Day, which from Milton, Middleton, Webster, or Augustine. I mean so far as the functioning of the poem is concerned." (Quoted by Hugh Kenner, *The Invisible Poet: T. S. Eliot*, W. H. Allen, 1960, p. 131.)

The emotional unity of the poem is indeed what matters. The form of the poem was, and certainly would have been without Pound's intervention, fragmented. The poem, being the work of genius, and as such mirroring important aspects of the truth of Eliot's age, an age without unity or centre, and in which the notion of sequential time had been abolished, could not but be a fragmented, kaleidoscopic entity, only held together by the consciousness of the poet. This was exactly what was happening in other aspects of the arts. Painters no longer painted representations or imitations of nature; they painted the pictorial equivalences of experiences which involved the whole being of the artist whose imagination was holding together various disparate, and even contradictory, aspects of timeless moments. Neither painters nor poets any longer believed in telling sequential stories. Paintings and poems were composed of juxtapositions or oppositions of various elements or collages having the same function as quotations in a poem, whose connecting link was the consciousness of the artist.

Eliot has denied what was said by some critics, namely that the poem expresses the disillusionment of a generation, and he has described such a judgment as nonsensical. The mood of *The Waste Land* is, in fact, present in all the poems which he wrote before the war. In contrast with the shallow optimism of those who could not sense the horror of the coming catastrophe of the Great War, Eliot felt that Western civilization had become mechanical, dehumanized, dull, dingy, and was best imaged by smelly streets and restless nights in cheap hotels. Corruption, degeneracy, greed, pure materialism were the main features of Western civilization. Princess Volupine, Sweeney, Burbank, Bleistein represent nothing else; and to them must be added the armaments-makers, the militarists and the moneymakers. All these people are hollow, disembodied ghosts, living in an age of superstition and unease, in which the sensitive person, and Eliot was extremely sensitive, could only be distressed and torn between irony and despair—the despair of Pascal, which Eliot described admirably, and which is also his own. He says that Pascal's despair "is in itself more terrible than Swift's, because our heart tells us that it corresponds exactly to the facts and cannot be dismissed as mental disease. . . . I know of no religious writer more pertinent to our time." (*Essays Ancient and Modern*, Faber, 1936, pp. 152–158.) None, of course, except Baudelaire, whose desperate awareness of original sin, and of good and evil, was the true basis of faith. As such awareness did not exist, or barely existed, at that time, there was no possibility of communication, or of true feelings, between human beings. Friendship was reduced to a faithless smile, and a shake of the hand, and sexual relations to purely mechanical, meaningless gestures. Still, in spite of this desolation and emptiness, the poet, the Fisher King of *The Waste Land*, does not finally despair, though life without faith is only appearance: a combination of atomic particles which do not make communication between one entity and another possible, and which cannot participate in any kind of organicity. The mind is a closed prison, and what it preceives is only appearances; there is no reality in a world of "hollow men". In this broken, fragmented world, the poet is the meeting point of all sorts of sensations, but he cannot connect or integrate them; he can only "shore them as fragments against his ruin".

*The Waste Land* reflects this fragmentation, and exhibits a medley of fragments, quotations from various languages, subjects of conversation, metaphors of disparate elements, images of sharply juxtaposed sensations or of interpenetration of the senses, in which the self or the apprehending subject is dissolved. A street becomes a sea in which people are drowned, and perceptions and knowledge become a complex awareness of relationships between emotions, sensations and thoughts. Eliot binds up his picture by selecting the fragments which are typical of the various aspects of modern life, and these fragments are mechanical, repetitive and unconnected. They are tea-cups, coffee-cups, stale smells, smoke, fog, inane crowds, social poses and attitudes, dreams and nightmares, about which it is easy to say, as Prufrock does, "I have known them all already, known them all".

*The Waste Land* is composed of five parts, subdivided into movements. The first part is entitled *The Burial of the Dead*. The poem begins with a sharp rejection of the widely accepted notion that April is a beautiful month, the month of growth and awakening of life. April is, on the contrary, the cruellest month, because it awakens us from our winter torpor, in which we had temporarily forgotten our dissolution in a world adrift.

> April is the cruellest month, breeding
> Lilacs out of the dead land, mixing
> Memory and desire, stirring
> Dull roots with spring rain.
> Winter kept us warm, covering
> Earth in forgetful snow, feeding
> A little life with dried tubers.

In medieval times, in ages of faith, April and Spring were the time of pilgrimages to holy places. Now, in our times, we go like the whirlwind through European towns, part of official tours, seeing nothing and ever carrying with us our "own emptiness and boredom". "Summer surprised us, coming over the Starnbergersee"; and these rich idlers, whoever they may be, related or not to the famous archduke of the Mayerling story, have the illusion of being free in the mountains; they read much of the night, and go south in winter in search of the sun. They are like all idlers, like Violet, in *The Family Reunion*; they have no other occupation except that of trying to fill up time.

The next movement, following this picture of restlessness, begins with the unavoidable and very disturbing question:

> What are the roots that clutch, what branches grow
> Out of this stony rubbish? Son of man,
> You cannot say, or guess, for you know only
> A heap of broken images, where the sun beats,
> And the dead tree gives no shelter, the cricket no relief,
> And the dry stone no sound of water.

Western civilization—what Pound described as "an old bitch gone in the teeth"—is only a heap of broken ruins and broken images, burnt out by the sun in a world without shadows, and above all without the purifying, life-giving water of faith. What does "Son of man"—Adam perhaps—think of this? If he has the courage to come under the shadow of the red rock, he might discover another shadow, a shadow which will fill him up with fear—the lurking shadow of death. "I will show you fear in a handful of dust." This echoes Hamlet's famous lines about "the noble dust of Alexander found stopping a bung-hole" and "the dust of Caesar might stop a hole to keep the wind away". (*Hamlet*, V, 1.) From this profound meditation on the insignificance of life and death, we pass to a striking, personal and also human experience—the experience of love:

> 'You gave me hyacinths first a year ago;
> 'They called me the hyacinth girl.'

This is a moving picture, in a kind of Ophelia-like world and situation, and whatever has happened, and whether the experience was pure ritual or love, it must have been something strong, with a mystical flavour, and it is something lasting, for she says:

> I was neither
> Living nor dead, and I knew nothing,
> Looking into the heart of light, the silence.

The third movement, dealing with Madame Sosostris, the clairvoyant, is more abstruse and sibylline than any other part of the poem. Madame Sosostris is the Cassandra of the modern age; in spite of her cold, and her fear of the police, she is the wisest woman in Europe, and her role is obviously important. With a wicked pack of cards, and without the help of any gods, who no longer exist, she can tell everybody's fortune. Phlebas, the sailor, described with the Shakespearian words, "those are pearls that were his eyes", had already been drowned in the poem *Dans le Restaurant*, and he will reappear again in the *Death by Water* section. The exact composition of the Tarot pack of cards which Madame Sosostris uses is, as Eliot says in his note, difficult to describe. "The Hanged Man, a member of the traditional pack, fits my purpose in two ways: because he is associated in my mind with the Hanged God of Frazer, and because I associate him with the hooded figure in the passage of the disciples to Emmaus in Part V. The Phoenician Sailor and the Merchant appear later; also the 'crowds of people', and *Death by Water* is executed in Part IV." (*Collected Poems 1909–1935*, Faber, 1936, pp. 78–79.)

The last movement with beautiful lyrical passages begins with a reminiscence of Baudelaire:

> Fourmillante cité, cité pleine de rêves,
> Où le spectre en plein jour raccroche le passant . . .

and switches over to Dante's *Inferno*, which is mirrored by the hollow, hopeless life of a metropolis in which men are like ghosts:

> I had not thought death had undone so many.
> Sighs, short and infrequent, were exhaled,   ·
> And each man fixed his eyes before his feet.

Whether in London or in Paris, life is the same; it is, as Baudelaire put it in *Voyage à Cythère*, "un désert rocailleux troublé par des cris aigres". The poet himself is part of this world, and the "Stetson" whom he apostrophizes is either someone from the inferno or the crowd itself. Mylae suggests the Punic Wars, therefore "Stetson" is someone from the past, and the corpse which he has buried in the garden is fear, eternal fear, which the Dog—conscience—could dig up again, and this would confront everyone with his own spiritual failing. This no one wishes to do, for everyone is in the same boat and shares the same feelings, including the reader: "Hypocrite lecteur!—mon semblable,—mon frère!"

Part II, *A Game of Chess*. In a game of chess, kings and queens can be placed near knaves and common people, as the needs of the game arise. So, from the Shakespearian beginning of evoking Queen Cleopatra and the chair—or the barge— she sat in, we end with the pub scene in which it is made clear that the preoccupations of common people are not very different from those of queens or rich ladies. Eliot seems to have made use here of the Mallarmean device of describing exactly all the details of a given scene which is under his eyes. One cannot help thinking of Mallarmé's poem, *Surgi de la croupe et du bond*, which is the description of a vase in Mallarmé's room. The queen, or the wealthy lady of the poem, sits at her mirror decorated with figures of Cupidon, with glass candelabras reflecting their light on the ceiling, among the dazzling sparkle of her jewelry; and the whole thing, bathed in perfumes and various scents and unguents, composes a kind of frozen, arrested world. In this very artificial world, the impression of artifice, or of what Baudelaire would have described as "suranné", is reinforced by the presence of a painting which is a sylvan scene representing:

> The change of Philomel, by the barbarous king
> So rudely forced; yet there the nightingale
> Filled all the desert with inviolable voice
> And still she cried, and still the world pursues,
> 'Jug Jug' to dirty ears.

John Lyly had already heard her voice and modulated her cry:

> O 'tis the ravished nightingale.
> Jug, jug, jug, tereu, she cries,
> And still her woes at midnight rise.

With Eliot, Philomel no longer tries to say "Tereus" or "tereu", as in John Lyly's poem; she says: " 'Jug Jug' to *dirty* ears". The phonetic sounds are very similar, the semantic connotations are unheroic and befitting the twentieth century.

This picture is a stump of time, together with other stumps of time, time past and lifeless in this hushed room, in which the silence is suddenly broken by the sound of footsteps on the stairs. They are the footsteps of the lady's husband, or lover, and with them one passes from a stilted artificial world, and from ancient myths, to modern conversations and the preoccupations of domestic strife:

'My nerves are bad to-night. Yes, bad. Stay with me.
'Speak to me. Why do you never speak. Speak.
  'What are you thinking of? What thinking? What?
'I never know what you are thinking. Think.'
. . .                                                'Do
'You know nothing? Do you see nothing? Do you remember
'Nothing?'

True enough, the questioned person remembers nothing, except
a Shakespearian line: "Those are pearls that were his eyes."
This Shakespearian tag is so elegant, but it does not allay
boredom, or offer much comfort to the lady who asks again:

  'What shall we ever do?'
                         The hot water at ten.
  And if it rains, a closed car at four

—in order to go for a drive, to accumulate more inane distractions and frustrations, or to keep tight closed eyes which
cannot sleep, while waiting for the knock of terror, the knock of
death on the door.
  We move, abruptly, without transition, in a fashion to which
Eliot has already accustomed us, from the richly scented,
lavishly furnished, yet barren and frustration-laden bedroom of
a queen or of a well-to-do lady, to a plain pub, where the talk
is not about carved cupids or raped Philomel, but about hot
gammon, false teeth and abortion; all that interspersed with or
rhythmed by the repeated calls from the publican: "HURRY
UP PLEASE IT'S TIME." Yet, all in all, this world is not
very different from the other. They both are, in fact, barren,
materialistic and totally deprived of true feelings. Albert has
been away for four years at the war, and if he does not get *it*
from Lil, he will get it from someone else, and Lil had better
make herself a little more attractive, in order to hold Albert.
No need of perfume, aphrodisiacs or expensive scents, only a
new set of teeth to improve a countenance much impaired by
repeated abortions and the unwanted birth of little George.
The same chemist will supply *them pills*, as he supplies the lady
of the burnished chair with perfumes. It's all the same to him,

c                          65

it's all the same to everyone—boredom, drinks, copulation, abortions and hopelessness, all fading away into the same general good-night.

Part III, *The Fire Sermon*, makes the theme of the poem explicit. Eliot says so himself in the note about Tiresias. That theme is self-consuming, sterile passions, confirmed by references to Buddha and to St. Augustine. Besides, it contains the most accomplished, the most beautifully controlled passage of poetry of the whole poem: it is the passage concerning the typist. *The Fire Sermon* begins with a description of the River Thames, which plays a central part in it. The river's tent of trees is broken; it could be autumn, the last leaves, like drowning fingers, sink on the wet bank; the nymphs of the river have departed, past loveliness is gone: "Sweet Thames, run softly, till I end my song." The Thames of Spenser is deserted; and not only the nymphs but also the modern city directors have all gone, perhaps to the waters of Leman: "By the waters of Leman I sat down and wept . . ." says the *I* of the poem, perhaps the poet himself, who was, indeed, by the waters of Leman, and in a very sad state. But he returns to the Thames with Marvell's famous view about time: "But at my back in a cold blast I hear", not "Time's wingéd chariot", but the rattle of bones, and a rat, vividly described as creeping upon the vegetation, while he was fishing and musing about other waters—the Shakespearian waters of *The Tempest*, in which Ferdinand's father was supposed to have been drowned. So he can see "white bodies naked on the low damp ground", and bones in a garret, while at his back he hears, not Marvell's chariot, but the horns and the sound of a motor bringing Sweeney to Mrs. Porter. This passage is reminiscent of a few lines from a little-known Elizabethan poet, John Day:

> When of the sudden, listening, you shall hear
> A noise of horns and hunting which shall bring
> Actaeon to Diana in the spring,
> Where we shall see her naked skin. . . .

Mrs. Porter and her daughter wash their feet in the moonlight; that brings to mind a line from Verlaine: "Et O ces voix d'enfants, chantant dans la coupole!" and memories of Philomel. We are back to the "unreal city" under the brown fog of a winter noon, not dawn, and with Mr. Eugenides, a Middle-Eastern man making a pederastic proposal.

Then comes the most beautiful passage, beginning with:

> At the violet hour, when the eyes and back
> Turn upward from the desk, when the human engine waits
> Like a taxi throbbing waiting. . . .

The human being is nothing more than a mechanical engine, and Tiresias, through whom we know the story and its meaning, Tiresias who has been both man and woman, and who has already lived this story, time and time again, sets the scene about the typist returning after work to her little flat where her drying combinations, "perilously" spread at the window, are touched by the sun's last rays. A faint glow of comedy lingers around these details and comments, and this will, therefore, prevent us from taking the story too tragically. Besides, nobody, none of the protagonists, does so; it is all mechanical. It is not experience, it is purely instant action, without past or future. Eliot in his notes to *The Waste Land* quotes the extract from Ovid's *Metamorphoses*, in which it is related that Tiresias underwent a change of sex for watching the coupling of snakes. This is presumably the occasion on which he "foresuffered" what is tonight re-enacted on this same divan bed. This same note says that "Tiresias is the most important personage in the poem", and that what he sees is, "in fact, the substance of the poem". The point is that Tiresias foresees and endures all, but does nothing about it. He merely is a passive sufferer and knower, but he is incapable of any reaction. The depth of psychological insight, the memorableness of this scene is conveyed in a language and a diction which admirably fit all the aspects of the action. The regularity of the lines, the alternate rhymes, all combine to convey the mechanicalness of the scene which ends with the four lines which illustrate the perfect identity of content and form, and sum up the meaning of the episode:

When lovely woman stoops to folly and
Paces about her room again, alone,
She smoothes her hair with automatic hand,
And puts a record on the gramophone.

The next line: " 'This music crept by me upon the waters' "
is lifted from *The Tempest*, and it brings us back to the Thames
and to the communal pub life teeming on its banks, and to the
Ionian white and gold splendour of St. Magnus Martyr. There
follows the song of the Thames' daughters, full of Wagnerian
overtones. The Elizabeth and Leicester episode is taken, as
Eliot suggests, from Froude's *Elizabeth*, volume I, chapter IV.
The frolics of Elizabeth and Leicester are not quite the same
as those of the typist and the young man carbuncular, but they
are of the same nature; they are mechanical and barren. So are
the happenings with the nymphs of the Thames, or with modern
girls being laid supine, on the floor of canoes, without comment
or resentment. The line:

Highbury bore me.   Richmond and Kew
Undid me

is reminiscent of Dante: "Siena mi fe, disfecemi Maremma";
and on Margate Sands, where Eliot wrote part of *The Waste
Land*, the song says:

I can connect
Nothing with  nothing.

From there, the scene shifts to Carthage where Augustine came
"burning, burning", like most of the characters of *The Fire
Sermon*, in his unholy lust for the flesh, and where he cried, "O
Lord Thou pluckest me out". The burning continues, and no
one notices it, because the time has not yet come.

Fire can burn and destroy as well as cleanse and purify;
water can also both fructify, give life and take life. In Part IV,
*Death by Water*, it only takes life, and the audience or the
reader, Gentile or Jew, is asked to "Consider Phlebas, who was
once handsome and tall as you", and has now forgotten, in his
grave of waves, the cry of sea-gulls and the problems of profit
and loss, and has entered the whirlpool of eternal transformation.

The fifth part of *The Waste Land*, *What the Thunder said*, obviously begins with Gethsemane and Golgotha and with the last night of Christ. The fount of life is now dead, and the so-called living are slowly dying, and it is *we*, the readers and speaker, who are all in the same situation; and we are so, until the speaker reassumes his separate identity to ask the question: "Who is the third who walks always beside you?" After the night in Gethsemane there is only the desert without water:

> Here is no water but only rock,
> Rock and no water and the sandy road. . . .

Everything is dried up, including sweat; everything is decayed, sterile, lifeless, and there is only fear. If only there were water, everything would change. Thence the allusion to the Journey to Emmaus, and the possible presence of Christ:

> —But who is that on the other side of you?

> What is that sound high in the air
> Murmur of maternal lamentation. . . .

The murmurs and lamentations are obviously those of the women of the city of Jerusalem, which was destroyed by barbarian hordes swarming over the plains. These hordes destroyed and destroy not only Jerusalem but also other centres of civilization, Athens, Alexandria, Vienna, London, where the poet is—unreal city—where he describes again a woman at her dressing table:

> A woman drew her long black hair out tight
> And fiddled whisper music on those strings
> And bats with baby faces in the violet light
> Whistled, and beat their wings
> And crawled head downward down a blackened wall
> And upside down in air were towers
> Tolling reminiscent bells, that kept the hours
> And voices singing out of empty cisterns and exhausted wells.

The crystals of *A Game of Chess* have turned into bats with baby faces, towers are upside down "tolling reminiscent bells", and voices sing, or rather croak, out of empty cisterns and wells. All this composes a picture of utter desolation, a kind of purgatorial world. After all these trials, the pilgrim, the Fisher King, reaches at last the Chapel Perilous of the quest, on the very edge of the world: "Only a cock stood on the rooftree" —perhaps the very cock which reminded St. Peter of his betrayal, or summoned Hamlet back to the end of night and to reality. Then, at long last, "a damp gust bringing rain", and the thunder speaks in the most primeval of languages: DA— give, and *Datta*—given.

> *Datta*: what have we given?
> My friend, blood shaking my heart
> The awful daring of a moment's surrender. . . .

—the moment of grace which brings faith, the only moment by which we can be aware of our existence, for it is only in such moments that we are in contact with God, and such moments are not found in our obituaries,

> Or in memories draped by the beneficent spider
> Or under seals broken by the lean solicitor
> In our empty rooms. . . .

Not only give, says the thunder, but "sympathize", understand others; get out of the prison of yourself, and meet others who are imprisoned by others, or imprison themselves in their pride, like Coriolanus. The boat responds to the giving, and to sympathy, and at last the Fisher King reaches the shore, and the journey eastward, across the desert, is ended. What will he do? "Shall I at least set my lands in order?" He ought to, but how can he proceed towards this good work? For the moment, all he remembers is part of a nursery rhyme: "London Bridge is falling down, falling down, falling down", a quotation from Dante, talking about the Provençal poet, Arnaut Daniel, whom he meets in Hell and who pleads with him not to be forgotten:

> Sovegna vos a temps de ma dolor
> Poi s'ascose nel foco che gli affina*

—a scrap of the *Pervigilium Veneris*, a scrap of a Tennyson line: "O swallow swallow, could I but follow", and a quotation

---

\* "Remember in due time my suffering;
Then he disappeared into the fire which refines."

from a poem by Nerval, *El Desdichado*: "Le Prince d'Aqui-
taine à la tour abolie"— a poem of dreams and magic horizons.
These scraps of memories, a summing-up of European life and
civilization, are all that remains in his mind: "These fragments
I have shored against my ruins. . . ." This is followed by a
quotation from Kyd's *Spanish Tragedy*, "Why then Ile fit you",
and by the conclusion that Hieronymo, the poet, is mad again;
and the poem ends on a note of hope with the words Give,
sympathize, control, and a repetition of the word Peace, peace,
peace, which is the ending of an *Upanishad*.

The sick soul in quest of faith, the Fisher King in quest of
water and lost virility, after going through the most desolate
aspects of Western life which are uprootedness, fruitless lust,
impotence, lost faith, mechanical love without feelings, finally
reaches the moment of surrender and the possibility of salvation. *The Waste Land* is in verse what *Ulysses* is in prose: a
complete synopsis of the psychological oscillations and conflicts
which raged in the soul of man in the first half of this century. Tiresias, as both man and woman, blind seer who has seen
everything, who has endured all and who knows past and
present, embraces with his empty gaze London's bridges and
Dante's inferno, as well as the amorous sport of Cleopatra, of
Elizabeth and of the twentieth-century typist. All these ghostly
characters seem to rush about aimlessly, making empty gestures, in a barren land in which the only use to which the water
has been put is to drown Phlebas, the bearer of the Holy Grail.
On such a land, every birth is worse than death, for the
Hanged Man has not yet appeared, and will not appear until
*Ash Wednesday* and *Four Quartets*.

*The Hollow Men.* "The most significant of all Eliot's poems,
from a confessional point of view, is *The Hollow Men*", says
Herbert Read (*T. S. E.—A Memoir*; published in *T. S. Eliot:
The Man and His Work*, edited by Allen Tate, p. 34.) It was
written in 1925, the year of religious crisis, and it could very
well be an overflow or a left-over from *The Waste Land*, for
not only is it suffused with the same type of despair or *angst*,
but it recreates vividly through its rhythm the failure to live

truly, which *The Waste Land* seeks to convey. The poem's first epigraph, "Mistah Kurtz—he dead", suggests Eliot's increasing affinities with Conrad, whose descriptions of London life are akin to his own. The second epigraph, "A penny for the Old Guy", is even more important for the understanding of the general meaning of the poem. It refers to that well-known Jacobean gentleman who had decided to make history by blowing up the House of Commons on 5th November, but because he was unwilling to kill some of his friends in the process, he allowed them to be warned, and so was caught and put to death. Thus, what was supposed to have ended with a bang merely ended "with a whimper". Since then, his death has become the object of a yearly ritual which is obviously a kind of substitute for religion and for the pagan midsummer bonfires that in Catholic countries take place on the feast of St. John.

If Guy Fawkes had "fared forward", without thinking, or trying to mitigate the impact of his action, he might have succeeded; but he belongs to the world of those for whom "between the conception and the creation falls the shadow". Therefore nothing ever happens; in such cases we are not in the world of action, we are in the limbo world where there is no action, in fact in one of the circles of Hell in which Dante placed the poet Sordello, not for doing but for not doing. It is also interesting to note, purely for the understanding of the English psyche, that a non-event, a failure, has become an object of national commemoration and rejoicing.

The poem begins with the words:

> We are the hollow men
> We are the stuffed men;

"we" are all involved, and we do not belong to

> Those who have crossed
> With direct eyes, to death's other Kingdom

—whom we ask to:

> Remember us—if at all—not as lost
> Violent souls, but only
> As the hollow men,
> The stuffed men.

We are in death, in a dream kingdom, a twilight world where nothing happens; there are only the remains of civilization and voices singing in the wind. The speaker is neither alive nor dead; he is merely an appearance, a mock cross, clad in dead rats' coats and crows' skins, to scare other rats or crows, and to be an example for others who lead the same life. We are back to *The Waste Land*:

> This is the dead land
> This is cactus land
> Here the stone images
> Are raised, here they receive
> The supplication of a dead man's hand
> Under the twinkle of a fading star.

Death no doubt has some other kingdom, a kingdom which souls have reached by truly facing death and not a kingdom where they are neither alive nor dead, a kind of in-between, a purgatory, in which they repeat over and over again the same empty gestures:

> The eyes are not here
> There are no eyes here. . . .

And we shall remain sightless, unless

> The eyes reappear
> As the perpetual star
> Multifoliate rose
> Of death's twilight kingdom

which is

> The hope only
> Of empty men.

So, the hollow men go round the prickly pear, round and round without any hope of redemption or of justification for a past which does not seem to exist. What they may have done or undone does not seem to matter. In fact, the explanation prompted by the sequence of stanzas which follows is that they have constantly failed to do anything:

Between the idea
And the reality
Between the motion
And the act
Falls the Shadow
> *For Thine is the Kingdom*

Between the emotion and the response, between the desire and the spasm, always falls the shadow. Lack of will, impotence, or misplaced scruples, as in the case of Guy Fawkes, are the causes of this incapacity to act. Yet there is a faint glimmer of hope:

> *For Thine is the Kingdom*

and

> *Life is very long. . . .*

# IV

## ASH WEDNESDAY

*Ash Wednesday*, which was first published in the *Saturday Review* in 1927, marks a definite turning point in Eliot's poetry.' It is a poem of resignation and acceptance, an assertion of faith found and held with anxiety, and an urge to rise to a higher sphere of being, through the shedding of desires, ambitions and the pressures and demands of the senses. It is not one single sequential poem, but a series of poems around one single theme or central emotion.

The poem begins on the mode and rhythm of Guido Cavalcanti's *Ballad*: *Perch'io no spero di tornor gia mai*—

> Because I do not hope to turn again
> Because I do not hope
> Because I do not hope to turn
> Desiring this man's gift and that man's scope
> I no longer strive to strive towards such things
> (Why should the agéd eagle stretch its wings?)
> Why should I mourn
> The vanished power of the usual reign?

The liturgical rhythm is that of a prayer, the music has a Tennysonian fluidity throughout.

> Because I know I shall not know . . .

The construction is syllogistic, Victor Hugoesque or Shakespearian, that is to say, it conforms to the rules of rhetoric which apply to the sonnet-form, or to any type of poetry or argument which passes from premises to a conclusion, and, in fact, delights in the required metaphysical skill of handling complex ideas:

I rejoice that things are as they are and
I renounce the blessed face
And renounce the voice
Because I cannot hope to turn again
Consequently I rejoice, having to construct something
Upon which to rejoice

And he passes freely from the personal, confessional tone, to
the generalized or congregational tone:

May the judgement not be too heavy upon us
. . .
Pray for us sinners now and at the hour of our death
Pray for us now and at the hour of our death.

The language is bare, but with extremely precise, vividly perceived images, close to natural speech and pervaded with the
gravity of church atmosphere. Eliot's use of images exhibits
two main characteristics. First, it is extremely precise, and for
such a concern with precision, there is no need to go to the
"imagists" to explain it. Eliot's great master, Dante, is the
most outstanding example in literature of extremely precise
and vivid imagery. Secondly, Eliot often uses very concrete
images accumulated during his childhood and youth on the
Atlantic coast where he only spent holidays, and these images depict
very exactly the landscape and the scenery as they truly are. The
*Quartets* abound in images of that nature, and the pattern generally
consists in passing from the personal to the general.

Having made these general observations about Eliot's imagery, one is bound to confess that the second section of *Ash
Wednesday*, which is what could be called a difficult poem,
contains images difficult to relate or to explain. Still, explanation is anything but necessary in poetry. What matters is the
experience which the poem conveys, and therefore the possibility of suggesting such an experience, so as to entice readers
to share it according to their own imagination and sensibility.
The lady is obviously the lady of Dante, some kind of mediat-
ing Beatrice who honours the Holy Virgin and has the power
to intercede for sinners. The juniper tree is the tree of death.
The three white leopards are difficult to explain, and it is not

necessary to do so; what is important is that they are three
beasts, or three major sins, and that they have devoured, dis-
sembled or disassembled the material components of the body
of the speaker. "Dissemble" means both "disguise" and the
opposite of "assemble". Only the bones now remain, and because of the goodness of the interceding lady, the bones,* the
essence, are redeemed and will shine in brightness and light.
The past, the senses, the indigestible portions which cannot be
transmuted by the three white leopards (being white, they must
be finally beneficent), are rejected. The lady is withdrawn in her
white gown, and the bones, cleansed, purified to whiteness, are
forgiven; the self is forgotten, and God said:

> Prophesy to the wind, to the wind only for only
> The wind will listen.

This lady,

> Lady of silences
> Calm and distressed
> Torn and most whole

—who unites all contrasts, who is also the rose, the rose of
Dante, the symbol of perfect union and mystical experience,
has supernatural powers and represents the final goal "where
all love ends", and once the redeeming death has taken place,
the true land can be reached:

> This is the land which ye
> Shall divide by lot. And neither division nor unity
> Matters. This is the land. We have our inheritance.

This is reminiscent of Ezekiel's vision of a valley full of bones,
"and lo! they were dry". This passage is like a song by St. John
of the Cross. It is pure music, and it conveys, beyond logical
explanation, the memory of an ineffable mystical experience
during which the soul has been enfolded in the rose of Eternity.

Section III comes back to the past, to a purgatorial climb,
from hell towards a vision of liberation. The atmosphere is
obviously Dantesque, and the fetid air and the devil on the

* The bones are sources of rebirth in ancient mythologies, particularly
among American Indians.

stairs are straight from the inferno. The speaker climbs on, and the vision of horror recedes, until, from the first turning of the third stair, he can hear music, and he can see a picture of enchanted rusticity and gay young love, expressed by the poet's usual imagery:

> Blown hair is sweet, brown hair over the mouth blown,
> Lilac and brown hair;

—and he continues to climb, hoping and longing for the call of the Lord, though he recognizes that he is not worthy of it.

In the fourth section, the speaker sees the lady, who is not quite the Holy Virgin, but who nevertheless wears Mary's colours and has performed miracles which, no doubt, would have transformed the Waste Land into a heavenly world; she has indeed

> Made cool the dry rock and made firm the sand
> In blue of larkspur, blue of Mary's colour,

and just as Arnaut Daniel, the Provençal poet, asked Dante not to forget, "Sovegna vos", she too is asked not to forget the years between, that is to say, the years of barren life, and to "redeem the time". Although she does not answer, she obviously does so; for

> . . . the fountain sprang up and the bird sang down
> Redeem the time, redeem the dream. . . .

Section V alludes to the search for truth, for the true word—Christ—and for the true land where wandering people could, at last, settle. The vision suggested is that of a prophet looking for a place of withdrawal, a place where there is perfect silence and where grace could be effective. Assailed by the usual doubts which follow the moment of vision, the prophet or quester asks:

> Will the veiled sister pray for
> Those who walk in darkness, who chose thee and oppose thee
> . . .
> Pray for those who chose and oppose. . . .

Will she pray for those who are terrified and cannot surrender, even at the last moment when they could do so, when they are about to enter the garden, which is heaven? Will they be able to renounce sin? We are back again to the haunted desert of *The Waste Land*, something which shows that, as in the case of the greatest mystics like St. John of the Cross, the true believer is never absolutely sure for long that he is perfectly attuned to God's grace. Far from being a poem of undisturbed certainty, *Ash Wednesday* is a poem of oscillations between heaven and purgatory, between anxiety and hope; it is a poem which describes exactly what it feels like to long for God, to have a vision of His glory, and to be filled with the terror of not being worthy of Him. True faith always walks the razor's edge of doubt and anxiety and never rests in solid, complacent certainty.

The sixth and last section begins not with "because", but with:

> Although I do not hope to turn again
> Although I do not hope
> Although I do not hope to turn
> Wavering between the profit and the loss. . . .

and the "twilight between birth and dying", while watching white sails flying seaward. This is an admirably concrete image which brings to mind the living imagery connected with the eastern Atlantic coast described in *The Dry Salvages*. After that, the *I*, the speaker, asks the Lord to bless him. This is followed by moving, rich, sensuous poetry laden with the subject's memories of past, sensuous experiences and poignant renunciation:

> The cry of quail and the whirling plover
> And the blind eye creates
> The empty forms between the ivory gates
> And smell renews the salt savour of the sandy earth. . . .

Standing on the threshold between a sensuous world movingly remembered, and a new world which opens up before him, he asks the blessed sister, the Holy Mother who is the Holy Virgin, to help him and to sustain him:

## *T. S. Eliot, Poet and Dramatist*

> Teach us to care and not to care
> Teach us to sit still
> Even among these rocks,
> Our peace in His will
> And even among these rocks
> Sister, mother
> And spirit of the river, spirit of the sea,
> Suffer me not to be separated
> And let my cry come unto Thee

—so that God's will might prevail, and "the garden where all love ends" might be found, "even among these rocks".

# V

## FOUR QUARTETS

*Ash Wednesday* is not a religious poem in the sense in which
Donne's religious sonnets are religious poems. It is a poem of
conflicts, conveying the struggle for liberation and the mystical
experience of a soul which thirsts for God and which has found
at last the union it was longing for. It marks the end of the
phase which began with *The Love Song of J. Alfred Prufrock*.
It does not mark the end of Eliot's growth of experience. Only
those who do not quite understand the true meaning of faith
can believe that once a human being has found God all his
problems are solved and he lives from then on in a state of
perfect bliss. God can be both found and lost, or half lost, and,
for those who truly believe, God is never held so solidly and
safely that one never has any fears of losing Him. The greater
the faith, the greater the anxiety of losing Him. Saints have
never lived in comfort, but in terror of not doing enough, or
of not doing the things God expected them to do, or the things
they should do in order truly to deserve His love and grace.
Eliot, ever open to experience, to doubt and anxieties, to the
sorrows and sufferings of his fellow men, and endowed with a
most acute and self-tormenting conscience, far from being
anaesthetized and made complacent by his hard-won, hard-
maintained faith, went on widening his field of experience,
assimilating and integrating all its component elements, until he
reached the sublime world of the *Quartets*, which undoubtedly
mark the zenith of his genius and are great poetry.

What was said about *Ash Wednesday* is even truer for the
*Quartets*: to call them religious poems would be to diminish
their scope and range, and to imply a conceptualism which is
alien to them. To say that this is the poetry of a devoutly
religious man is another matter. Eliot, the poet, did not write
to propagate or to illustrate a point, or an aspect of faith; he

wrote, as all true poets do, with his whole being, in moments when the guiding force or form seeking expression was not belief, but imaginative truth or experience, coloured and nourished by his beliefs, haunted or illumined by the vision which he sought to shape into a symbolic entity that would satisfy the high criteria of aesthetics and of his poetic genius intent upon making as clear as possible the truth which he had been allowed to glimpse. In the act of writing, it is the poet and not the religious man who is in control, and the poet writes not to propagate beliefs, but to render visible, for himself and for others, experiences or areas of truth which he himself discovers through poetic creation.

*The Quartets* contain the experience of a lifetime, but these experiences are indeed the moments, unattended or otherwise, which cut off from, or project life out of, Time, that is to say, out of everyday time. They belong to another category of time, that which Bergson described as "duration": *"la durée* toute pure", he said, "est la forme que prend la succession de nos états de conscience quand notre moi se laisse vivre, quand il s'abstient d'établir une séparation entre l'état présent et les états antérieurs. . . . Il suffit qu'en se rappelant ces états il ne les juxtapose à l'état actuel comme un point à un autre point, mais les organise avec lui, comme il arrive quand nous rappelons, fondues pour ainsi dire ensemble, les notes d'une mélodie." (Bergson, *Essai sur les Données Immédiates de la Conscience*, p. 84.) Duration is a moving present, continuing the past, preparing for the future. Our past is always with us, but we only know it in the present. "En réalité le passé se conserve de lui-même automatiquement, tout entier sans doute, il nous suit à tout instant; ce que nous avons pensé, senti, voulu depuis notre première enfance est là penché sur le présent qui va s'y joindre." (Bergson, *L'Evolution Créatrice*, p. 5.) References to Bergson, or to Bradley's *Appearance and Reality*, which Eliot had studied in detail, to Plato or to Indian philosophy, which he also knew admirably, do not mean that the *Quartets* are expositions, in varying degrees, of these philosophies.

A poet is not a philosopher in the sense that a philosopher is a philosopher. A poet's beliefs and thoughts are those which can be extracted from his poetry, and they only matter in as far as they have been integrated in his poetry and not as beliefs or thoughts *per se*, unless, of course, one deals with philosophy expounded in verse. The philosophy of a poet is what emerges from the contemplation and enjoyment of his poetry, which exists as an organic entity and not as an instrument to teach, to explain or to expound thoughts; therefore it must not be assessed as philosophy by philosophers, but as an emanation of the poetry by critics of poetry. Such an assessment should always be a matter of pragmatic observation starting from the poetry, and precluding the application of any systematic examination of it as pure and simple philosophy, or any confrontation with an *a priori* philosophic norm or system. If some kind of philosophic pattern emerges after such an examination, it should only arise from the poem, and it should be viewed as a *sui generis* mode of making symbolic representations of realities upon which to meditate, and not as a logical and analytical exploration of the truth.

Poetry and philosophy are two aspects of the discovery of truth and therefore of the growth of the human mind. Truth is eternal, but in order that its phenomenal aspects may be grasped in Time, it has to be expressed in entities which are apprehensible to the senses. Poetry and philosophy are both means of apprehending and expressing in different ways the truth, whose noumenon is unchanging but whose existential aspects are differently interpreted throughout historical time and according to individual sensibility. There are at least two broad ways of approaching truth—the intuitive and the rational—and even in the rational way of apprehending truth, there is at the beginning an intuitive moment which is rationalized, analysed and pursued throughout all its ramifications in the case of the philosopher, and expressed in sensuous, concrete terms in the case of the artist. Poetic truth, the revelatory power of words, has taken various aspects throughout the centuries. With the Symbolists—and here we come to the background of T. S. Eliot's poetry—the undefinable moment of poetic truth, the "thing in itself", can only be suggested or hinted at, without narrative elements or didacticism, through music, images and rhythms. With them we are back to the Platonic and Pythagorean concept of the world as musically constructed, and to the notion that essential truth is best suggested through the analogy of music apprehensible to the senses, bearing in mind, of course, the Platonic and early Christian concept that "unheard music is the music of Heaven". The analogy with music embraces both the human aspect of music embodied in the structure and surface aspect of the poem and the supra-human aspect embodied in the fact that the poem, in its essence, tends towards the moment of "music unheard", which is also the moment of union with God and absolute knowledge, at the intersection of Time with Eternity, Time being the becoming of Eternity.

*Four Quartets* are attempts through poetry, analogous to music, to rise to the "music unheard"—the timeless moment of Eternity. Although words are not musical notes, at the source of words and music there is rhythm or *mousike*, the *idea* which preceded both, and it is through rhythm in all its existential aspects—stress, tempo and quantity—that poetry approaches music. Each of the *Quartets* is constructed according to a pattern similar to that of a musical quartet. In each of them, with one exception, starting from a place in space and time, the poet tries to reach the internal song, the ideal point where poetry and music are one. In each case, through a process of exploration based on images and rhythms unfolding along a musical structural pattern, he tries to suggest and to reach a state of not being in Time, whence an experience of timelessness may be born. With the exception of *Burnt Norton*, which, being the first *Quartet*, is introductory to the theme and the most important in that respect, the *Quartets* are all connected with geographic locations, and to a certain extent with historical time; they all start with a projection from the present into the past and future which are one and which the poet brings to life from affective memory.

That means that the experience recalled and the feelings which were originally part of it emerge simultaneously as a whole, not separate or reconstructed intellectually. What happens in affective memory, which is the source of poetry, is an upsurge of feelings whence an emotional state as close as possible to the original one arises. The poet starts off from a state of practical timelessness or chaos and moves towards consciousness. It is Valéry's journey from chaotic dawn and non-being to light and life; it is Proust's journey "à la recherche du temps perdu", the journey in search of Time, which becomes transcendent through art.

The fact that *Four Quartets* proves that their author is a thinker as well as a poet, and that he is aware of the dominant trends of thought of his age and of past ages, does not mean that the *Quartets* are a conceptual poem or an intellectual creation. They are the various modes of an experience imaginatively lived and transmuted into poetic truth, and there is no reason whatever to confuse the dialectical and Heraclitean processes which the poet uses in order to convey the wholeness of an experience, in which intellect and feelings are one, with dialectics or with the analytical criticism of a poetic experience. The average person sees only one thing, and generally only one aspect of a thing at a time, but the man of extraordinary gifts, the man of genius, has the means to apprehend the ontological structure of the thing which he observes, and to become that very thing in order to reveal what it really is. Blake or Klee, for instance, could pierce the surface of the objects which they observed and reach to their essence and unicity. Eliot has an all-round vision which sees things with their various contraries, relationships and complementary elements, and with the criticisms pertaining to them, and all these aspects resolve themselves, through the dialectical fire of the imagination, into true poetic knowledge which takes place not in sequential time but in timeless moments of intuition which gather in themselves the simultaneity of all the attributes and relationships of the experience lived. Donne's dialectical process of exploring feelings and thoughts has been described as mere intellectual exercise by some who confuse descriptions of sentiments with true feelings; yet, with few exceptions, no other poetry is suffused with greater passion, human love and anxiety. There is passion in *Four Quartets*, not the passion of Donne, but the profoundly human, controlled passion of a man of imagination and sensibility who cares for his fellow-beings and for the plight and suffering of all those who have to endure Adam's curse.

*Burnt Norton* begins with a statement of the concept of Time which underlies *Four Quartets*. Present and past are both contained in time future, which is a projection of the past made from the present which is continuously becoming the past. Therefore, if the future is made of the past, it is also the past, and since both only exist in the present, there is neither future nor past; there is only the present, the continuous becoming which confers existence upon past and future and constantly transforms them. If we bear in mind the fact that consciousness is consciousness of something, we realize that each instant of consciousness takes place against a background of nothingness, and also that it creates nothingness. The instant of consciousness is therefore the meeting-point of nothingness and existence, and it rests upon a continuous inrush or tension towards consciousness, carried forward by what has been and what is to be, which continuously becomes the past, modifying the apprehension of what is already and of what is to be. Thus, the instant of consciousness is a continuously vain attempt to bridge an unbridgeable gap and to catch up with what cannot be caught up with, except by the abolition of consciousness through some kind of transcendental experience beyond cognitive knowledge or, one might suppose, through the death of the body. If there is only the present—the point of conscious apprehension of existence and continuous becoming—there is really no past, and Time is, as Eliot rightly says, unredeemable. What has been can never be altered and remains eternally the same; in the end there is no past, present or future, there are only two dimensions: the instant of consciousness and Eternity, which is both what is and what is not, being and non-being, and can only be apprehended in the present at the existential point where consciousness passes from Time into timelessness.

Therefore it is idle to speculate about what might have been, for what might have been, since it has not been, is not only beyond our knowledge, since it has not entered actual existence, but obviously had not to be, since it has not been; it has remained non-being and we can only know non-being through being, so that to talk about something which might have been, but has not been, is a pure intellectual game without existential foundation. In the end the "might have beens" we talk about are merely imaginative constructions, all based on things that have actually been, and not on fictitious might-have-beens. There is no true "might have been", for if a thing had the necessary positive potentiality for being, as is suggested by the conditional tense, it would definitely have been. We can add to the incomplete beauty of a sketch or to the incomplete life of an artist who has died young. We can talk, from a background of incomplete knowledge, about a thing which has not yet been and therefore might still be, but once a thing has been it seems meaningless to talk about what it might have been.

> What might have been and what has been
> Point to one end, which is always present.

Existence, which is the present, is the only way of finding out the worth of any "might have been".

What is the use, says the poet, of getting lost in the rose-garden which could be memory or the place where true reality dwells, lured by a fleeting thought or a bird? Still the attempt is made and the poet leads us back to the world of childhood, a world which is beyond the senses and in which "the roses have the look of flowers that are looked at", that is to say, a world in which objects give and receive and become part of the life of the subject: in short, a world of lived experience with perceptions and interpretations coexisting inseparably within a creative subject. The garden could be memory with its content grasped through consciousness in the present and fading away as soon as there is a loss of attention or of vision:

> Then a cloud passed, and the pool was empty.

Yet this garden could also be, as is very often the case with Eliot, who constantly mixes reality and imagination, a real garden or one which naturally existed once. In 1934, Eliot, holidaying at Chipping Campden, visited an uninhabited mansion erected on the site of an earlier house which had been burnt down, and he visited the deserted garden:

> Other echoes
> Inhabit the garden. Shall we follow?
> Quick, said the bird, find them, find them,
> Round the corner. Through the first gate,
> Into our first world, shall we follow
> The deception of the thrush? Into our first world.
> There they were, dignified, invisible,
> Moving without pressure, over the dead leaves,
> In the autumn heat, through the vibrant air,
> And the bird called, in response to
> The unheard music hidden in the shrubbery,
> And the unseen eyebeam crossed, for the roses
> Had the look of flowers that are looked at.

One can easily picture in this garden the ghosts of its former inhabitants, a festive occasion, people walking here and there in shrubberies with flowers being looked at. It also suggests "our first world", the world of childhood, to which we have access once we have come into life after having passed through "the first gate", and we can hear, through memory, the unheard music of these early days, and the deserted garden and the empty pool are brought to life by memory, which, through the present, holds them alive, but only for brief moments.

The second movement begins with the symbol of the wheel representing the universe or life, with its temporal and perennial elements respectively conjured up by garlic and sapphire:

> Garlic and sapphires in the mud
> Clot the bedded axle-tree.
> The trilling wire in the blood
> Sings below inveterate scars
> And reconciles forgotten wars.
> The dance along the artery,
> The circulation of the lymph,
> Are figured in the drift of stars. . . .

The images which follow suggest that life is one, that the life of the microcosm reflects the life of the macrocosm and that, in the end, all temporal contrasts will be finally reconciled into the perennial world of the stars, symbols of Eternity. Here we are at the very core of the poetic experience, at the point where individual consciousness has merged into the timelessness of the source of all things—the still point of the turning world:

> . . . at the still point, there the dance is,
> But neither arrest nor movement. And do not call it fixity.
> Where past and future are gathered.

Yet not the present: we have on the one hand Eternity, which is both being and non-being, stillness and movement, all contrasts resolved into silence, source of all things; and we have on the other existence in Time, the means of bringing to life the content of Eternity. "Only through time time is conquered"; only things which have existed in Time will be eternal, and only the present can bring to life "the moment in the rose-garden". The philosophical inference is that time past and time future allow but little consciousness, that is to say, offer but little awareness of existence, in fact they offer none except when apprehended in the present, and the apprehension of past and future is itself timeless; it is the means of lifting consciousness out of Time and of bringing Eternity into Time in moments of intensity or annunciations:

> But only in time can the moment in the rose-garden,
> The moment in the arbour where the rain beat,
> The moment in the draughty church at smokefall
> Be remembered; involved with past and future.
> Only through time time is conquered.

The third movement takes us into the underworld of the subway in London, and is meant to symbolize one of the worst possible worlds, a limbo world where men are neither dead nor alive, for they are acted upon like bits of paper in the wind. It is a world of animality in which the soul is reduced to its simplest expression, a "twittering world", kept from distraction by insignificant distractions:

> Neither plenitude nor vacancy. Only a flicker
> Over the strained time-ridden faces
> Distracted from distraction by distraction
> Filled with fancies and empty of meaning
> Tumid apathy with no concentration
> Men and bits of paper, whirled by the cold wind. . . .

What means of salvation can one find in such a world of contingencies and trivialities? The poet suggests the way he has already chosen, the way of renunciation in order to own, the way of divestment, of absolute poverty in order to possess, the way of solitude, silence and metaphysical despair in order to know, the way of expectation and concentration on the present, which at any moment might be the timeless moment of God. Socrates, the neo-Platonists, the Christian mystics, Yogi philosophers and Descartes himself, have all stressed the importance of the negative way in order to reach plenitude and affirmation, and of the willed concentration on the instant in the present in order to reach Eternity. They have all recognized the fundamental existential basis of the apprehension of Eternity, and the necessity of leaving behind the cloud of knowing so as to reach the night of unknowing or the void before there can be true knowledge and true life.

> Descend lower, descend only
> Into the world of perpetual solitude,
> World not world, but that which is not world,
> Internal darkness, deprivation
> And destitution of all property,
> Desiccation of the world of sense,
> Evacuation of the world of fancy,
> Inoperancy of the world of spirit. . . .

We must not forget that when Eliot wrote this, he was working at Faber's, in Russell Square, and living in Gloucester Road. To commute, as he did daily, between these two stations, he had to descend lower, to the lowest circle.

The fourth movement of the poem opens upon an intense moment of concentration and expectation. History and Time have faded into oblivion, the angelus bell has sounded away the day into a cloud; we wait anxiously, divested and bare, wondering whether Divine Grace will come down to earth. The light, with its last reflections on the kingfisher's wings, has died too. We wait, wondering whether we shall at last truly live. The difficulty remains in the end insuperable, as Mallarmé realized; for how can man reach "silence", metaphysical silence, source of all things, through the temporal means of the words?

## "Four Quartets"

> Words strain,
> Crack and sometimes break, under the burden,
> Under the tension, slip, slide, perish,
> Decay with imprecision, will not stay in place,
> Will not stay still.

The attempt is doomed to failure. Yet the final movement of the poem, pervaded with anxiety and hope, suggests a possible clue to the human plight; the possibility of salvation lies in love, the prime mover and goal of the movement which is life:

> Love is itself unmoving,
> Only the cause and end of movement,
> Timeless, and undesiring
> Except in the aspect of time
> Caught in the form of limitation
> Between un-being and being

—that is to say, caught in the moment of Divine Grace, the timeless moment rising from Time out of Time, the moment of revelation, the shaft of sunlight sustained by its own power while the sun, which is Time, has already disappeared. The poem closes on a final note of sadness about the rarity of such moments:

> Ridiculous the waste sad time
> Stretching before and after.

*Burnt Norton* contains in a highly concentrated form all the ideas and concepts which will be given flesh and blood in the following *Quartets* and which will culminate in the climax of sensuousness and moving beauty of *Little Gidding*, which is the ninth sphere of the poet's journey from earth to Heaven, from Time to timelessness. In the other three *Quartets* the various themes are taken up again and explored through rich imagery and in rhythms flowing smoothly into one another, and closely interrelated as if they were the movements of a sonata in which all the possible variations of the central musical phrase are worked out.

East Coker is a village in Somerset in which the Elyots lived, and from where Andrew Elyot emigrated to America in 1667. It is in the church of this little village that the ashes of its most illustrious son were laid to rest in 1965. The poem, *East Coker*, begins with a transposition of Mary Queen of Scots' motto which becomes "In my beginning is my end", a statement which is thoroughly deterministic and is fully illustrated by the explanations which follow. All things change and move according to an immutable pattern of cyclic rises and falls, births and deaths, which characterize the life of the earth as well as the life of mankind. In the end, the world will not find its true harmony until it returns to the Heraclitean fire, "which burns before the ice-cap reigns". Then, after a repetition of the motto which will only revert to its original form at the end, we have, as already mentioned, an exact description of the entrance to the little village of East Coker, so exact that on the only occasion when I went there, the sight of the village immediately brought back to memory the words which Eliot had used. This village produced another Elyot, a Sir Thomas Elyot, who in *The Boke named the Gouvernor*, in 1531, had described his native village "wherefore in the good order of daunsinge a man and a woman daunseth together". Eliot sees in his mind's eye the scene which must have taken place in the past, a scene which is part of the rhythm of nature and of human life, and in order to relate the scene to the past, he uses the old spelling:

> The association of man and woman
> In daunsinge, signifying matrimonie—
> A dignified and commodious sacrament.
> Two and two, necessarye coniunction,
> Holding eche other by the hand or the arm
> Whiche betokeneth concorde.

The movement ends with a striking coda:

> Dawn points, and another day
> Prepares for heat and silence. Out at sea the dawn wind
> Wrinkles and slides. I am here
> Or there, or elsewhere. In my beginning.

The daring construction, "Dawn points", which so aptly describes the sun's rays surging from the sea, seems to be more French than English, and shows the extent to which Eliot had assimilated the French language.

The second movement, after what the poet himself describes as "a periphrastic study in a worn-out poetical fashion," comes to grips with the problem of experience and knowledge, and the wisdom of old men who, in that Autumn of 1940, when *East Coker* was written, had obviously deceived us into a feeling of serenity which had shattered by war. Knowledge is the past, and the past is constantly modified:

> There is, it seems to us,
> At best, only a limited value
> In the knowledge derived from experience.
> The knowledge imposes a pattern, and falsifies,
> For the pattern is new in every moment
> And every moment is a new and shocking
> Valuation of all we have been.

The only wisdom we can acquire is that of humility, for

> The houses are all gone under the sea.
> The dancers are all gone under the hill.

They all go into the dark, however high or low their position in life may have been.

> Et la garde qui veille aux barrières du Louvre
> N'en défend point nos rois.

—said Malherbe about death, and it is the same for all men. So what kind of aspirations could men entertain? The reply is the reply of Buddha and the great mystics:

> I said to my soul, be still, and wait without hope
> For hope would be hope for the wrong thing; wait without love
> For love would be love for the wrong thing; there is yet faith
> But the faith and the love and the hope are all in the waiting.
> Wait without thought, for you are not ready for thought:
> So the darkness shall be the light, and the stillness the dancing.

This, the central idea of the poem, is perfectly expounded in the fourth and most beautiful movement, in which poetry rises to the purity and transparency of music. We recognize here once more the way of the neo-Platonists, of the early Christian mystics and of St. John of the Cross. We must accept pain which is part of living; the surgeon, in this case Christ or the holy man, wounded, as we all are, will try to save us. The nurse, the Church, dying as we all do, will try to mitigate Adam's curse; the whole of mankind is sick with Adam's sin which is the sin of the temporal world. The poet deliberately avoids any hint of religious symbolism or theological argument in a stark picture of decadence and decay which is carefully kept at a purely concrete level until, at the end, without preparation, we are suddenly confronted with a line which plunges us into the heart of religious experience and reveals to us that already before, in other times, mankind had reached similar straits and had been saved through the suffering of the God-man whose perenniality and immanence transcend human failings. There is only one way to rise to the eternal: through Divine Grace and through the suffering of Christ who dies for us every moment of our lives:

> The dripping blood our only drink,
> The bloody flesh our only food

—and in spite of His constant sacrifice, a repetition of His death in historical time, we call "good" the Friday which commemorates His death.

The final movement of the poem begins with an expression of regret about wasted years and about the difficulties of the poet grappling with his tasks:

> And so each venture
> Is a new beginning, a raid on the inarticulate
> With shabby equipment always deteriorating
> In the general mess of imprecision of feeling,
> Undisciplined squads of emotion.

And in the end, what is the use of such conquests, what is there to conquer? We all unfailingly move towards the same waiting home which is the one we start from and to which we return. There is only one attitude to adopt:

> We must be still and still moving
> Into another intensity
> For a further union, a deeper communion
> Through the dark cold and the empty desolation,
> The wave cry, the wind cry, the vast waters
> Of the petrel and the porpoise. In my end is my beginning.

Every moment of intensity is a new moment containing the whole past of man, modifying it and being modified by it; darkness is the darkness of God and through death man and God can be reconciled.

For Eliot, as for Pascal or St. Thomas Aquinas, faith is not obtained by a surrender of the intellect, but on the contrary through the intellect leading man to the final point where logic compels commitment to, and acceptance of, faith. A. N. Whitehead summed up this attitude by saying: "Religious truth must be developed from knowledge acquired when our ordinary senses and intellectual operations are at their highest pitch of discipline." The intellect, of course, may still prove difficult to keep under control, even once one has committed oneself to faith; yet, if that faith is strong enough to stand and to maintain alive a constant awareness of man's limitations and of his risks of eternal suffering without God's presence, it can bear all the restlessness of the intellect which can neither prove nor disprove it. One may approach God through mind, but as the author of *The Cloud of Unknowing* remarked, "one can only reach Him and hold Him by love". In his essay on Pascal, Eliot has pointed out that "despair is essential to the progress of the intellectual soul", for despair and transcended suffering are as much ways to God as purgatory is the transitional way to Heaven:

> If to be warmed, then I must freeze
> And quake in frigid purgatorial fires
> Of which the flame is roses, and the smoke is briars.

With *The Dry Salvages* (a small group of rocks off the North East coast of Massachusetts) we move to Eliot's childhood landscape and reminiscences of the Mississippi and the Atlantic coast. We are back to the theme of Time. The river symbolizes the Stream of Life and man as an individual, and also reminds him of his bondage to Nature; the sea is historical time and also Time itself. The sea, as Time, is indifferent to the fluctuations of history and tosses about indiscriminately "the shattered lobsterpot, the broken oar and the gear of foreign dead men".

The tolling bell of the sea is the bell which marks the end of historical cycles and civilizations; it is rung by passing storms and earthquakes. The human time is Bergsonian, it is the time lived, the duration which has nothing to do with the mechanical time of clocks; it is time felt by the human heart in intense moments, it is the time of women worrying and waiting between midnight and dawn for the return of their men who are out at sea, it is the time when future and past are fused in the intense moment in which the consciousness of existence is nothing but waiting, it is the moment

> ... when the past is all deception,
> The future futureless, before the morning watch
> When time stops and time is never ending. ...

The deterministic force of nature, which is Time, relentlessly, indifferently, continues to clang the bell marking changes. The ever-changing sea, the continuous recurrence of the events connected with it, well illustrate the meaninglessness of the cycles of life which only acquire meaning through annunciations or moments of pure consciousness or meeting points of Time and Eternity. We have calamitous annunciations, annunciations of terror which keep man open to God. We have the annunciation of death which transforms and brings man back to God, and we have had the great, historical Annunciation, the coming of God in Time—the corner-stone of Christianity. History's endless and meaningless cycles can only be redeemed by the instant of intensity and daring which repeats the historical Annunciation, the moment at which God and man are one, the moment when man in Time rises to the eternal through selflessness and Divine Grace.

The past is not sequential but simultaneous, it surges from memory in moments of sudden illumination which bring to life not only memories of past personal experiences but also memories of the whole human race, memories of all that has been and remains unchanged and unredeemable, since it is irreversible and varies in meaning according to the moment when one summons it back into lived experience:

> And the ragged rock in the restless waters,
> Waves wash over it, fogs conceal it;
> On a halcyon day it is merely a monument,
> In navigable weather it is always a seamark
> To lay a course by: but in the sombre season
> Or the sudden fury, is what it always was.

In the end there is no past or future, there is only Eternity and existence—the foundation of instants which can reveal Eternity.

> Here between the hither and the farther shore
> While time is withdrawn, consider the future
> And the past with an equal mind.
> At the moment which is not of action or inaction
> You can receive this: "on whatever sphere of being
> The mind of a man may be intent
> At the time of death"—that is the one action
> (And the time of death is every moment)
> Which shall fructify in the lives of others:
> And do not think of the fruit of action.

The moment which is not of action or inaction is the moment of waiting *intent* towards God, waiting for Him, without any ulterior motives whatsoever. But most of us are not able to render ourselves fit for such states when Divine Grace may come and transport us out of Time:

> But to apprehend
> The point of intersection of the timeless
> With time, is an occupation for the saint—
> No occupation either, but something given
> And taken, in a lifetime's death in love,
> Ardour and selflessness and self-surrender.
> For most of us, there is only the unattended
> Moment, the moment in and out of time,
> The distraction fit, lost in a shaft of sunlight,
> The wild thyme unseen, or the winter lightning
> Or the waterfall, or music heard so deeply
> That it is not heard at all, but you are the music
> While the music lasts.

When such moments come, all awareness of the individual self is abolished, existence becomes the divine music of Eternity, "or the simple flame, containing ingathered the scattered leaves of the universe".

> Here the impossible union
> Of spheres of existence is actual,
> Here the past and future
> Are conquered, and reconciled. . . .

Such moments are the sole aims of human life:

> And right action is freedom
> From past and future also.
> For most of us, this is the aim
> Never here to be realised;
> Who are only undefeated
> Because we have gone on trying

—and we must go on trying while accepting our fate with humility.

Little Gidding is a place in Huntingdonshire. The little chapel is a restoration of an earlier one. Cromwell's soldiers sacked it in 1647, and dispersed the community, which was High Catholic. Charles I took refuge there, after Naseby, "very privately in the dark of night". It is a place of prayer. After the Elyots' departure from East Coker, England, another Eliot, Thomas Eliot, returns with his newly discovered faith to a place in England where faith was once valid and is more than ever needed, since we are in the middle of the greatest catastrophe the world has ever known—the Second World War. *Little Gidding* is Eliot's masterpiece. His control of the fluidity of the four-stress line, the perfect harmony between the word and the soaring meditation which embraces some of the most moving aspects of human experience, from concrete reality to the highest mystical elevation, carry the reader through various metamorphoses, and deposit him transformed on distant shores waiting and longing for the lost vision to return again. He has known timelessness, he has been through the rose-garden or felt upon him the ineffable shaft of sunlight which heralds timelessness and the abolition of the self.

The poem begins with the most striking opening of contrasts which resolve themselves through a melody of images melting into one another, explaining the meaning of the "zero summer":

> Midwinter spring is its own season
> Sempiternal though sodden towards sundown,
> Suspended in time, between pole and tropic.
> When the short day is brightest, with frost and fire,
> The brief sun flames the ice, on pond and ditches,
> In windless cold that is the heart's heat,
> Reflecting in a watery mirror
> A glare that is blindness in the early afternoon.

Then, after this remarkable flight of imagination, we suddenly come back to reality, to a given place as perfectly recognizable as East Coker. If you came this way, whether you were a broken king or a plain everyday traveller, you would find it, for it is well described, but you would also find it if you were in search of faith, for it is a sacred place, a place where prayer has been valid, and will be so for all time. There are other places of pilgrimage, on promontories, in cities or islands.

> But this is the nearest, in place and time,
> Now and in England.

But one would come here, or rather the poet says, you would come here, not to question or verify, but to pray, and this is followed by the second movement of the poem, which is a most sustained flight of lyricism, a violin solo piece, with all variations resolved, with each stanza ending with a refrain which brings in the four elements. The concrete and the imaginary are constantly and perfectly blended; the notion that it is only from time that timelessness can be reached is repeatedly asserted, and we clearly realize that "dust in the air suspended" marks, indeed, all that may remain of a house destroyed by aerial bombardment:

> Ash on an old man's sleeve
> Is all the ash the burnt roses leave.
> Dust in the air suspended
> Marks the place where a story ended.

> Dust inbreathed was a house—
> The wall, the wainscot and the mouse.
> The death of hope and despair,
>    This is the death of air.

This lyrical passage composed of eight-lined, rhymed stanzas heralds the magnificent encounter of the poet with a ghost, a friend, during a night when he was patrolling the streets of London as an air raid warden. This passage, which Eliot himself described as a tribute to Dante, cost him endless pains, and is the high point of the poem. It is analogous to Dante's meeting in Hell with his master Brunetto Latini, and it is written in *terza rima*, with alternances of masculine and feminine rhymes. The German bombers, the "dark dove with the flickering tongue", have passed below the horizon of their homing, and the poet patrolling the desolate streets encounters many ghosts: Mallarmé's, Hamlet's, ghosts of his past, and the ghost of Yeats, who had died and had been buried on distant shores, in France, and with whom he holds a most moving conversation:

> And he: 'I am not eager to rehearse
>    My thought and theory which you have forgotten.
>    These things have served their purpose: let them be.
> . . .
> But, as the passage now presents no hindrance
>       To the spirit unappeased and peregrine
>       Between two worlds become much like each other,
> So I find words I never thought to speak
>       In streets I never thought I should revisit
>       When I left my body on a distant shore.
> Since our concern was speech, and speech impelled us
>       To purify the dialect of the tribe
>       And urge the mind to aftersight and foresight,
> Let me disclose the gifts reserved for age
>       To set a crown upon your lifetime's effort.
>       First, the cold friction of expiring sense
> Without enchantment, offering no promise
>       But bitter tastelessness of shadow fruit
>       As body and soul begin to fall asunder.

Second, the conscious impotence of rage
  At human folly, and the laceration
  Of laughter at what ceases to amuse.
And last, the rending pain of re-enactment
  Of all that you have done, and been; the shame
  Of motives late revealed, and the awareness
Of things ill done and done to others' harm
  Which once you took for exercise of virtue.
  Then fools' approval stings, and honour stains.
From wrong to wrong the exasperated spirit
  Proceeds, unless restored by that refining fire
  Where you must move in measure, like a dancer.'
The day was breaking. In the disfigured street
  He left me, with a kind of valediction,
  And faded on the blowing of the horn.

The third movement of the poem absorbs such ghosts into renewed patterns. King and Roundheads are all parts of the same world, and there is no sense in trying to ring bells backward or in summoning the spectre of a rose, whatever rose it may be:

These men, and those who opposed them
And those whom they opposed
Accept the constitution of silence
And are folded in a single party.

The fourth movement celebrates the refining fire, the fire of terror descending from above, and the only way one can be redeemed from the concrete fire of egoism and self-love is through the fire of pure love, the love of God.

We only live, only suspire
Consumed by either fire or fire.

The fifth movement reverts to *East Coker*'s problem of beginning and end, the use of words and the problem of Time. All actions are of equal duration; they all lead to the same place. We all go the same road, only the moments which take us out of time matter, and only true love can do that. So love is both the torment and the salvation, for love is the *primum mobile* of creation, the main attribute of God. Self-love is the worst perversion of God's gift, a perversion which God has to redeem through His Grace. The connection or rather the necessary interrelation between Time and Eternity is once more stressed:

> The moment of the rose and the moment of the yew-tree
> Are of equal duration. A people without history
> Is not redeemed from time, for history is a pattern
> Of timeless moments.

A people without a history is a people without any meeting points with Eternity, therefore a people condemned to nothingness. History is a pattern of the instants which link up the temporal with the eternal; any moment in existence could be the foundation of such instants, so history is now, always now; it is in England, but it could also be somewhere else, as long as it is the instant which transcends existence. Yet in the end, there shall be an end to Time, which shall return to Eternity:

> And all shall be well and
> All manner of thing shall be well
> When the tongues of flame are in-folded
> Into the crowned knot of fire
> And the fire and the rose are one.

The concept of Time exemplified in *Four Quartets* is, as previously noted, in one way Bergsonian, with its stress on the simultaneousness of the past always on the verge of becoming the present, which brings it to life in moments of intensity in which the human being is aware of being transformed in a process of continuous becoming. On the other hand, this notion of Time, which is practically Platonic, is also essentially Christian. There is no contradiction between the Bergsonian stress on duration as a means to reach an awareness of existence and the Christian stress on the instant of grace and illumination as a means to reach Eternity.

Christian thought, from Duns Scotus and St. Thomas Aquinas to Kierkegaard or T. S. Eliot, is above all existential. Everything takes place in Time: sin, redemption, and God Himself accepted, up to a point, to live and die in Time. Christian thought rests, first and foremost, on the reality of the instant in Time which places man in the context of Eternity.

The whole strength of human pathos is concentrated on the memory of, or on the expectation of, such instants.

This is the concept which marks the most fundamental difference between certain aspects of Platonism and Christianity. For Plato, such instants could not exist and they could not even be thought of, for he would not admit of any possible contact between Time and Eternity. Christianity marks, on the contrary, the complete marriage between Time and Eternity. It is in Time that the Christian decides on his Eternity; Time is therefore immanent. The instant of Eternity is the instant of absolute plenitude, and the existent can only think of Eternity as the future, which is a memory of the Edenic past. Nietzsche sought to discover Eternity in the recurrence of things. Kierkegaard sought to discover the recurrence of things in Eternity, and he believed in the continuous integration of past and future in the present which, with the exception of a more marked stress on the importance of the past, was very close to Bergsonian duration.

For Christianity the fundamental relationship between Time and Eternity is embodied in the Incarnation, the union of God with one man at a given moment and place in Time, during which the contingent became eternal and history was eternalized. The instant eternalized is the true foundation of Christianity; Eternity for the Christian is based on an historical fact, it has an inescapable existential basis. In Christian thinking, there is no separation between the temporal and the eternal. Yet, only Divine Grace can bring about such a union, so the Christian lives in a constant state of anxiety. The one who needs it most, the sinner or Satan, is the one who is most anxious for it; therefore he is in some ways the one who is nearest to God. The anxiety caused by the nearness to God can be so unbearable that even Christ on His last night could not bear it, and He asked for His Father's help.

The modern concept of Time, the concept which seems to be that of *Four Quartets*, whether Christian, Bergsonian or Einsteinian, is essentially two-dimensional. It is neither Cartesian nor Hegelian; it is neither the immanentism with transcendence in abeyance of the former nor the abstract idealism of the latter; it is Time as the becoming of Eternity apprehended in moments of grace or genius through individuated existence; and the concept of Time is the most fundamental aspect of human sensibility.

The *Quartets* are a whole universe in which the deep Christianity of the poet no doubt plays a part, but they are a synthesis of various thoughts, religions and elements. Air, water, earth and fire, glimpses of paradise, of purgatory, of hell, are involved together with visions of suffering, death and the wisdom of Christian faith and Hindu philosophy. All this forms a whole, a fully integrated, mature world, in which a poetic sensibility of the first order has reached its zenith. This sensibility holds together various world views and relates them to previous poetic moments which the poet has lived. The heavenly moments of the hyacinth girl, the whispers of children's voices of *Marina*, the rose, the garden, they all recur and are sublimated in the poet's journey towards some form of earthly liberation and sainthood, culminating in "the crowned knot of fire", in which "the fire and the rose are one", of *Little Gidding*. This integration, this union of composite, conflicting Heraclitean elements, is achieved through love, but love in the highest possible sense; it is the love which unites the dead and the living, the earth and heaven, and which is the very force which animates the world, therefore the love which transforms and maintains life and relates the living and the dead.

There are perhaps greater poets; that is a debatable, though hardly a profitable, point; but this is one of the highest peaks of modern poetry: a universe subsumed in music and words, a complex of vital metaphysical experiences and visions, held together and fused into oneness by one of the most self-critical and conscious imaginations. St. John of the Cross, Donne, Julian of Norwich, and also "one who died blind and quiet", to say nothing of Christ and Krishna, cast shadows across these poems, but the one which hovers over it all the time is that of his most lasting master, Dante, whose *Divine Comedy* Eliot's own work reflects on a smaller scale, from the Hell and purgatory of *The Waste Land* and *The Hollow Men*, to the Paradise of *Little Gidding*.

# VI

# *ARIEL POEMS* AND THE FIRST DRAMATIC WRITINGS

*Journey of the Magi* was written in August 1927 as a result of a commission by Faber's for a poem to be included in a series of one shilling greeting cards entitled *Ariel Poems*. The first five lines are taken from the Christmas sermon of Bishop Lancelot Andrewes (1555-1626), whose tricentenary Eliot had celebrated with an article published in the *Times Literary Supplement* in 1926, and reprinted later in a book of essays entitled *For Lancelot Andrewes*. It is worth quoting the passage in question: "It was no summer progress. A cold coming they had of it at this time of the year, just the worst time of the year to take a journey, and specially a long journey in. The ways deep, the weather sharp, the days short, the sun farthest off, *in solstitio brumali*, 'the very dead of winter'." Eliot has made use of exactly the same images, the same words and the same method of proceeding and progressing with his narration. This method is sustained throughout, with stops and starts—exposition of details, memories of cast away moments, re-capitulation of the present situation and judgment of this current venture:

> At the end we preferred to travel all night,
> Sleeping in snatches,
> With the voices singing in our ears, saying
> That this was all folly.

The writing is streamlined, sparse, carrying no extra weight, as befits the theme of such an arduous journey, and it shows the perfect control of the medium he is using, a medium which is already shaping towards the dramatic poetry he was dreaming of. After their trials, the Magi came to a kind of heaven-like valley with three trees, a white horse and

> ... a tavern with vine-leaves over the lintel,
> Six hands at an open door dicing for pieces of silver ...
> And arrived at evening, not a moment too soon
> Finding the place; it was (you may say) satisfactory.

This scene is pregnant with symbolism which for the moment eludes the Magi. They have arrived at the end of their journey in a kind of earthly paradise, a place which shows kindness to old animals (the white horse), but which also contains three trees already waiting for their load, the leaves of the true vine, and hands "dicing for pieces of silver"—something which will be used later. The scene is clearly set, but the hidden meaning eludes them. They can hardly remember the whole thing, but whatever remains in their minds, they don't want it forgotten; so they say:

> ... but set down
> This set down
> This: were we led all that way for
> Birth or Death?

There was a birth, which was at the same time a death, the death of the Magi, the end of their own religion. So they go back to their own kingdom "with an alien people clutching their gods". The Magi have not quite grasped what is about to happen, but they have been deeply disturbed, and they sense that only death can bring forth the true kingdom.

After *Journey of the Magi* Eliot wrote *A Song for Simeon*, which corresponds to previous poems like *The Waste Land* and, especially, *Gerontion*. One will never stress enough the point that Eliot's poetry forms a whole, with certain recurring themes unfolding organically like a tree, and a continuously develop-ing style, and this is, to me, one of the hallmarks of great poetry. His poetry is throughout interrelated not only in themes, but also in the fact that many passages were originally intended for one poem and were later fitted into another. *The Waste Land* and *Ash Wednesday* are examples of such a method. *Ash Wednesday* is also connected with *Journey of the Magi*, with

106

*Marina* and, above all, with *Burnt Norton*, particularly the fourth section, the meditation in the garden, and the fifth, the meditation in the wood. Then there is not only the inter-relatedness of the poetry, but there is also the interrelatedness of the plays with the poems, particularly the first two plays, *Murder in the Cathedral* and *The Family Reunion*, which contain conscious echoes of *Burnt Norton*. All this means that he is a great poet, and that, though his work can be anthologized or apprehended piecemeal, its importance and worth can only be grasped by treating it as a whole.

*A Song for Simeon* is a very explicit parallel to *Gerontion* and to *Journey of the Magi*; it is in three parts. Lord, says Simeon, we are in the heart of winter, which is also my own winter:

> My life is light, waiting for the death wind,
> Like a feather on the back of my hand.
> Dust in sunlight and memory in corners
> Wait for the wind that chills towards the dead land.

"Like a feather on the back of my hand," he is all light, ready waiting for the call of the Lord; he is the opposite of Gerontion—"an old man in a dry month" waiting for the winds which will toss him about only once he has been reduced to, or dissolved into, his component atoms. Simeon has not been tossed about by the winds; he has led a sedentary life in his native city, which he knows well, and where he has led the good life: "There went never any rejected from my door." He is eighty years of age, and he asks God to let him die:

> Before the time of cords and scourges and lamentation
> Grant us thy peace.
> . . .
> Grant Israel's consolation
> To one who has eighty years and no tomorrow.
> According to thy word.
> They shall praise Thee and suffer in every generation
> With glory and derision,
> Light upon light, mounting the saints' stair.

Simeon is tired, tired and old, but he neither longs for martyrdom, nor for the ultimate vision; he just wants to die, like the Moses of Vigny, who is also tired, and he begs God to allow him to sleep the sleep of the earth. No heroics, no rhetoric, just the plain prayer of a tired, good, old man, who has accomplished his task on earth and who hopes for God's salvation.

*Animula* is another *Ariel* poem. Its first line, " 'Issues from the hand of God, the simple soul' ", is a quotation from Dante's *Purgatory*: "From the hands of Him who loves her before she is, there issues like a little child that plays, with weeping and laughter, the simple soul, that knows nothing except that, come from the hands of a glad creator, she turns willingly to everything that delights her." (*Selected Essays*, p. 260.) The simple soul, compared to a child, is also reminiscent of Baudelaire's poem: "Pour l'enfant amoureux de cartes et d'estampes. . . ." This little child, the soul, lives in a world of happy confusion between fancy and reality, in pleasant, well-to-do surroundings; he barely distinguishes between "is" and "seems", and in case of doubt or worry, quickly seeks refuge behind the *Encyclopaedia Britannica*:

> Issues from the hand of time the simple soul
> Irresolute and selfish, misshapen, lame,
> Unable to fare forward or retreat,
> Fearing the warm reality, the offered good,
> Denying the importunity of the blood. . . .

This child, this incarnation, seems to lead a very tame life, and at the end of the poem the lives of Guiterriez, obsessed by speed and power, and of Boudin, blown to pieces—both victims of science—seem to be equally dull and in need of being redeemed by prayer and grace.

*Marina* is also an *Ariel* poem, and it was published in 1930. It is one of the most beautiful, if not the most beautiful of Eliot's short poems. The epigraph is from Seneca's *Hercules furens*, who has slain his children in a fit of madness. The name "Marina", a very poetic, evocative name, is from Shakespeare's *Pericles, Prince of Tyre*, and it belongs to one of the most moving heroines that Shakespeare ever created. Pericles, her father, pursued by some kind of curse from a wicked king whom he has offended, is shipwrecked with his wife, who has just given birth to a daughter. From all appearances they are both lost; in fact they manage to reach the shore, and once she has grown up, the daughter, Marina, is put in a brothel, where her beauty and virtue are such that they abash and turn away all would-be customers. The aged Pericles, searching for his lost daughter, discovers her at last, together with his wife, whom he had presumed dead, and in finding his lost daughter he has found again his soul. The poem begins with the striking image:

> What seas what shores what grey rocks and what islands
> What water lapping the bow
> And scent of pine and the woodthrush singing through the fog
> What images return
> O my daughter.

When he finds her, he says:

> What is this face, less clear and clearer
> The pulse in the arm, less strong and stronger—
> Given or lent? more distant than stars and nearer than the eye

—and in his imagination he hears:

> Whispers and small laughter between leaves and hurrying feet
> Under sleep, where all the waters meet.

—whispers of children's voices, always symbols of happiness in Eliot's poetry, and the sounds of their feet emerging from water whence his daughter has herself emerged, transformed, recreated, so that the hope is that little children, dream-children, might perhaps now come. The passage—

> Bowsprit cracked with ice and paint cracked with heat.
> I made this, I have forgotten
> And remember.
> The rigging weak and the canvas rotten
> Between one June and another September.

—is very Coleridgean, and could suggest the suffering which Pericles has inflicted upon himself and which he has endured. He has not only made his own suffering; he has also made, or created, both his dream-child and his child, which will carry the new life with "the awakened, lips parted, the hope, the new

ships". So we have an entrancing vision of hope reborn, of life
continuing and moving towards wide horizons, and this makes
acceptable the fate of Pericles or of the speaker of the poem.
Whatever may happen to him, now he has found again his redeeming daughter, "the hope, the new ships". This is a most
moving poem, full of magic and music, in which the mastery of
style entirely matches the depth and richness of the experience
conveyed.

*Sweeney Agonistes* is subtitled *Fragments of an Aristophanic
Melodrama.* It carries as an epigraph two quotations—one from
*The Choephoroi,* which reads:

> *Orestes:* You don't see them, you don't—but *I* see them: they
> are hunting me down, I must move on.

—the other from St. John of the Cross:

> Hence the soul cannot be possessed of the divine union, until it
> has divested itself of the love of created beings.

The first quotation explains Sweeney's irrepressible urge to rid
himself of an obsession by narrating it. He has got a fit of
terror, and, like Harry in *The Family Reunion,* though he may
or he may not have done the deed which haunts him, he must
exorcise it through words:

> I gotta use words when I talk to you
> But if you understand or if you don't
> That's nothing to me and nothing to you . . .

He must speak; after that, again like Harry Monchensey, he
may go, God knows where, and live free from the fears and
terrors he has left behind.

Eliot always believed that a poet should necessarily turn his
activity towards drama. When he began to think about it in
the nineteen-twenties, he felt that the music hall was at that
time the only source of dramatic vitality, and he had a great
admiration for its leading performers—Marie Lloyd, George
Robey, Nellie Wallace and Little Tich. With drama, he always
wanted to reach a large public. He therefore "wanted to write a
drama of modern life about furnished-flat sort of people, in a

rhythmic prose, and perhaps with certain things in it accentuated by drum beats".* And he wanted to elevate these scenes of everyday life to the level of ritual. The Greek theatre was the best way to provide the kind of support or substratum for this aim, and *Sweeney* was going to be "an Aristophanic melodrama". *Sweeney* was interrupted and put aside unfinished. It reappears in *The Family Reunion*, under another name, while the Greek theatre provides the substructure of four of Eliot's plays: *The Oresteia* for *The Family Reunion*, *Alcestis* for *The Cocktail Party*, *Ion* of Euripides for *The Confidential Clerk*, and *Oedipus Coloneus* for *The Elder Statesman*.

*Sweeney Agonistes* is in two parts. The first part, *Fragment of a Prologue*, begins with a dialogue between Dusty and Doris in their furnished flat, the rent of which is being paid by a certain Pereira, who is no gentleman but is probably a wealthy South American. Sam would be a much better companion, for he is a gentleman, but he has obviously no money, so Pereira will have to do; but for the moment they do not wish to see Pereira, they want to stay by themselves, out of the world, dreaming of their future with a pack of cards. Still, they are not quite out of the world, for there is a telephone, which rings to announce Pereira, who is successfully fobbed off with the excuse of a sudden temporary illness. So, back to the cards, to the tarot, to read from them what the future will be. The first card, the King of Clubs, could be Sweeney, or Pereira, says Dusty. Then, an old friend whom we have already met in *The Waste Land*, Mrs. Porter, is mentioned; there, she was connected with Sweeney, for whom she was waiting. Doris is not Madame Sosostris, but "she has got a touch with the cards". Then suddenly the two of spades turns up, and that means the coffin and death; but whose death will it be? Who knows?— or rather, as Doris puts it, "You've got to know what you want to know", and "It's no use asking more than once". This sounds as implacable as Fate or Destiny. Fortunately, they are saved by the arrival of the Knave of Hearts, Sam Wauchope, with three friends admirably named Horsfall, Klipstein and Krum-

* Hugh Kenner, *The Invisible Poet: T. S. Eliot*, 1960, p. 179.

packer, the latter two being Americans, who are going to be shown around London by Sam.

The second part, *Fragment of an Agon*, brings in Sweeney, whose first words to Doris are:

> I'll carry you off
> To a cannibal isle

—and this isle is no Gauguinesque island of dream; rather it seems a terrifying place where Sweeney, obviously disillusioned with life, waits or hopes to reach a different state of being. He does not propose to live with Doris; he proposes to eat her, once she has been duly transmuted into a "missionary stew". She will, therefore, be part of a ritualistic death, like that of Celia in *The Cocktail Party*, and she will be a means of getting rid of the body and of being divested of the love of created things, as the second epigraph of the poem suggests, in order to reach higher spheres of being. She will be taken to an island where there is nothing to see except palm trees one way, and the sea the other way, and where life is absolutely nothing but "birth and copulation and death"; and Sweeney adds:

> I've been born, and once is enough.
> You don't remember, but I remember,
> Once is enough.

Sweeney has obviously had his awakening, and, like the Magi, he is no longer at ease in the old dispensation; he knows that life is death. That is indeed the answer which he gives to the "bamboo song", which is in praise of a life of pleasure:

> Life is death
> I knew a man once did a girl in

—and not only that, says Sweeney:

> Any man might do a girl in
> Any man has to, needs to, wants to
> Once in a lifetime, do a girl in.

Is he himself that man? Is he, like Harry Monchensey, the guilty one, or is he merely part of the love of horror which the public enjoys through stories of women being done in, cut to pieces, dissolved, dispersed, burnt, etc.? Whether Sweeney's story is true or not does not matter; he is not concerned with the exact meaning of words. He says he has got to use them, but he must not be taken literally; he is intent on conveying an experience about which he is not very sure himself. Whether it is real or imaginary. Sweeney himself is involved in the experience, is part of the narration, and cannot therefore judge whether it is true or false:

> But I've gotta use words when I talk to you.
> But here's what I was going to say.
> He didn't know if he was alive
>             and the girl was dead
> He didn't know if the girl was alive
>             and he was dead
> He didn't know if they both were alive
>             or both were dead
> If he was alive then the milkman wasn't
>             and the rent-collector wasn't
> And if they were alive then he was dead.
>         . . .
> When you're alone like he was alone
> You're either or neither
> I tell you again it don't apply
> Death or life or life or death
> Death is life and life is death . . .

You become obsessed by your story, and:

> You dreamt you waked up at seven o'clock and it's
>             foggy and it's damp and it's dawn and it's dark
> And you wait for a knock and the turning of a lock
>             for you know the hangman's waiting for you.
> And perhaps you're alive
> And perhaps you're dead
> Hoo ha ha

So we are left in the same state of not knowing as in the case of the exact whereabouts and end of Harry, in *The Family Reunion*. What he has done, only he, and perhaps not even he, knows. He is locked up in his own incommunicable world of which we can only see a transparency and some reflections.

This was an experiment in versification by the greatest master of the age in the art of metrical virtuosity. There were other fields to explore. Eliot was anxious to do so, and in 1934 he agreed to write a pageant-play to be given at the Sadlers Wells Theatre in the same year. This was *The Rock*. It provided him with the handling of another type of verse with which he had not yet experimented—choric verse; and it was an experiment which he made use of in his first two plays. The normal line of dialogue in Eliot's plays and in a large amount of his poetry is the three- or four-stress line, which he uses with great flexibility. The choric line fulfils a purpose different from the dialogue line. It is not primarily meant to convey meaning; it is meant to be spoken by a chorus, and it is meant to keep to a certain rhythm which must be clearly established and sustained, and which therefore cannot afford subtle variations of pace and tone. On the other hand, it must avoid monotony, by varying the length of the lines used and the length of the units of speech. Yet, it is evident that in spite of all the possible skill involved, it can hardly avoid becoming a kind of chant, and as such, it must be used sparingly, unless it happens to coincide with a certain vogue, as was the case in the early nineteen-thirties. *The Rock* was a great success. George Bell, Bishop of Chichester, came to see the performance, and he asked Eliot if he would write a play to be performed for the Canterbury Festival, in 1935. The play was to run for one hour and a half. Eliot accepted, and the result was *Murder in the Cathedral*.

# VII

## THE PLAYS

Before examining in detail Eliot's five plays, it seems to me
useful to say a few words about the problems which confronted
him when he began to write poetic drama, and which he consciously endeavoured to solve. Although "poetic drama" and
the so-called well-made play are now out of fashion and have
given way to naturalistic slices of life, pornography, happenings, audience participation, communal creativity, dramatized
documentary, living theatre, improvised theatre, etc., the nineteen-twenties and nineteen-thirties, and even up to the nineteen-
fifties, witnessed a marked reaction from nineteenth-century
naturalism, and a serious attempt to revive poetic drama. The
attempt was anything but a failure; the great names of
Yeats, Synge, O'Neill, Claudel, Brecht, Eliot and Beckett, to
quote only a few, show the extent to which the attempt was
successful. By the time Eliot began to write, after Yeats and
Synge, he realized, as Brecht had put it, that this was no time
for heroes. He realized also that this was the age of the common man, who expressed his jumbled up emotions and his fragmented apprehensions of reality in racy, colloquial, syncopated,
associational types of speech. He understood that the main
failure of late nineteenth- and early twentieth-century verse
dramatists was a linguistic failure. They had sought to use a
form of historical verse which, deprived of substance, sounded
hollow and artificial, and they had dealt with themes which had
no impact on modern sensibility. Ibsen had solved the problem
by repudiating verse, and Eliot felt, wrongly perhaps, that both
he and Chekhov had restricted their dramatic range by using
prose instead of verse. "There are great prose dramatists—such
as Ibsen and Chekhov—who have at times done things of which
I would not otherwise have supposed prose to be capable,
but who seem to me, in spite of their success, to have been

hampered in expression by writing in prose. This peculiar range of sensibility can be expressed by dramatic poetry, at its moments of greatest intensity. At such moments, we touch the border of those feelings which only music can express. We can never emulate music, because to arrive at the condition of music would be the annihilation of poetry, and especially of dramatic poetry. Nevertheless, I have before my eyes a kind of mirage of the perfection of verse drama, which would be a design of human action and of words, such as to present at once the two aspects of dramatic and of musical order." (*Selected Prose*, p. 85.)

Having said that, he makes it clear that he believes that "the poetry of a great verse drama is not merely a decoration of a dialogue of a drama which could, as drama, be as well put in prose". He believes, on the contrary, that "it makes the drama itself different and more dramatic", and that verse, as a dramatic medium, is superior to prose: "To work out a play in verse is to be working like a musician as well as like a prose dramatist; . . . the verse dramatist must operate on you on two levels at once, dramatically with the character and plot . . . [and] underneath the action, which should be perfectly intelligible, there should be a musical pattern which intensifies our excitement by reinforcing it with feelings from a deeper and less articulate level. Everybody knows that there are things that can be said in music that cannot be said in speech, and things that can be said in poetic drama that cannot be said in speech." Verse was, therefore, according to Eliot, a prerequisite of poetic drama, and it had to be a type of verse which would avoid the echo of Shakespeare, for "I was persuaded", said Eliot, "that the primary failure of nineteenth-century poets when they wrote for the theatre (and most of the greatest English poets had tried their hand at drama) was not in their theatrical technique, but in their dramatic language; and that this was due largely to their limitation to a strict blank verse which, after extensive use for non-dramatic poetry, had lost the flexibility which blank verse must have if it is to give the effect of conversation. The rhythm of regular blank verse had become too remote from the movement of modern speech. Therefore what I kept in mind was the versification of *Everyman*, hoping that anything unusual in the sound of it would be, on the whole, advantageous." (*Idem*, p. 77.) The point is clear: Eliot's main aim was to avoid the use of a verse which was part of the "high style" and of heroic drama which he did not wish to write. His task was Wordsworthian: a return to everyday speech, a shearing off of the decorative, pictorial and static elements which, whether eighteenth-century or Georgian, had, at their worst, turned poetry into a kind of refined product remote from life and which men could only indulge in when they were dressed in their Sunday best.

The need to harmonize dramatic verse with common language is, of course, practically as old as tragedy itself, and Aristotle had already noted that "in the theatre one has to use a type of verse which sounds least like verse, which mingles more easily than the others with common speech". Eliot has tried to base his rhythms upon common speech and to evolve a form of verse which can command all the resources of language. It is basically a flexible verse with three primary stresses, a caesura, possible secondary stresses and a varying number of syllables. It is a loose three-stress line which has obviously benefited from Hopkins' theories about sprung rhythm, and which leaves plenty of scope for rhetoric and for variations according to the effective weight which it is made to carry. It can be tightened up and given the taut muscularity required to carry emotions by restricting the secondary stress and the number of syllables, or it can be loosened up and made to sidle along with prose when there is no intensity to convey. It is above all a functional line, Racinian in its transparency and avoidance of unnecessary images and metaphors. It is a line highly suitable for the themes in which speech must be based on everyday, living rhythms, and in his later years it seems to have reached the same stage as the Alexandrine, in which the rhetorical stress is more important than the strictly metrical stress.

Eliot showed very early in his career that he was greatly concerned with the possibility of restoring poetic drama to the stage. By 1924, he had already stated that he wanted to write a drama of modern life in rhythmic prose. In fact, his vocation as a dramatist is part of his vocation as a poet, and he certainly did not turn to drama because he had exhausted his lyrical vein. Besides that, lyrical poetry itself is always dramatic in the sense that it underlines the separation of the singer from the state of things as they are, as they have been or as they might be, and Eliot's genius embraces meditative and humorous poetry as well as orthodox dramatic poetry. His aim was to reinstate poetic drama on the stage, and in order to do that: "poetic drama . . . must . . . enter into overt competition with prose drama. As I have said, people are prepared to put up with verse from the lips of personages dressed in the fashion of some distant age; they should be made to hear it from people dressed like ourselves, living in houses and apartments like ours, and using telephones and motor cars and radio sets. Audiences are prepared to accept poetry recited by a chorus, for that is a kind of poetry recital, which it does them credit to enjoy. And audiences (those who go to a verse play because it is in verse) expect poetry to be in rhythms which have lost touch with colloquial speech. What we have to do is to bring poetry into the world in which the audience lives and to which it returns when it leaves the theatre; not to transport the audience into some imaginary world totally unlike its own, an unreal world in which poetry is tolerated." (*Idem*, p. 79.)

Eliot was an extremely conscious artist who knew what he wanted to do, and who had the genius and the patience to pursue his aim to what he considered a satisfactory end. His aim was to win for poetic drama the place which it no longer held with the average theatre public. He did not attempt, like Giraudoux or Anouilh, to modernize myths through the use of topical language, situations and characters, and neither was he laboriously Freudian in the style of O'Neill in *Mourning becomes Electra*. What he did was to weave modern, everyday situations into the framework of an ancient myth and then to deepen these situations down to the point where, through the transparency of the naturalistic surface, shines the immanent, perennial reality of affective truths which are valid for all men at all times. Being a religious writer in the sense that he was constantly concerned with the interplay of immanence and transcendence, whether he disguised his pursuits under secular terminologies and analogies or used straightforward Christian symbolism and references, Eliot was always in search of the kind of truth which relates his dramatic characters to the society to which they belong, and, beyond that, to a God-made creation.

He used Greek myths in his last four plays, and in some instances he has so well covered up his tracks that, had he not declared his debt to the Greek dramatists, probably no one would have discovered it. Whether it is a comedy like *The Confidential Clerk* or a serious drama which, though it ends with death, as in the case of *The Cocktail Party*, is also a kind of comedy, the naturalistic surface of the situations and of the characters always casts out long shadows which plunge deep into the perenniality of human life. Eliot is in this respect both Ibsenian and Strindbergian. His "naturalism" is a complex structure of essential traits and elements acting as a façade to hold the attention of the audience, which, more often than not, finds itself unexpectedly out of its depth, and which, once it has regained the shore, spends its time trying to discover, with the help of very ingenious critics, how it was lured away towards the open sea and the depths, where it caught a frightening glimpse of the hidden reality that is a reflection of "le Dieu caché".

There are those who think that there was a falling off of poetry after *Murder in the Cathedral*, and that Eliot, in trying to bring poetry to the stage, in fact arrived empty-handed on it, and therefore made a fruitless journey. This is not so; for such a judgment presupposes, on the one hand, a lack of conscious planning and intention, and on the other, a desire to bring back to the stage a caparisoned, highly-plumed muse whom everybody would recognize at once. This was never Eliot's aim. In his lecture on Yeats, delivered in 1940, he said: "But another, and important, cause of improvement is the gradual purging out of poetical ornament. This, perhaps, is the most painful part of the labour, so far as the versification goes, of the modern poet who tries to write a play in verse. The course of improvement is towards a greater and greater starkness. The beautiful line for its own sake is a luxury dangerous even for the poet who has made himself a virtuoso of the technique of the theatre. What is necessary is a beauty which shall not be in the line or the isolable passage, but woven into the dramatic texture itself; so that you can hardly say whether the lines give grandeur to the drama, or whether it is the drama which turns the words into poetry." (*On Poetry and Poets*, p. 259–260.)

Being extremely clear-sighted about his aims and about the conception of his work, he carefully explained in *Poetry and Drama* what he was trying to do, what he thought he had achieved and what he thought he had failed to do. It should be sufficient to say that after *Murder in the Cathedral* he was fully aware that, although he had certainly achieved something in taking his first steps in poetic drama, he had done so with the help of so many props and the use of so many already well-practised movements, that this merely proved that he could walk the path of poetic drama which, for the moment, had led him nowhere.

The voice of Becket is the voice of a man "who does not hope to turn again", whatever the temptation, including that of the fourth tempter who offers him the crown of martyrdom:

> Fare forward to the end.
> All other ways are closed to you
> Except the way already chosen.
> . . .
> King is forgotten, when another shall come:
> Saint and Martyr rule from the tomb.
> Think, Thomas, think of enemies dismayed,
> Creeping in penance, frightened of a shade;
> Think of pilgrims, standing in line
> Before the glittering jewelled shrine,
> From generation to generation
> Bending the knee in supplication.
> Think of the miracles, by God's grave,
> And think of your enemies, in another place.
> . . .
> Seek the way of martyrdom, make yourself the lowest
> On earth, to be high in heaven.

The main problem of the play is that Becket is a man who has heard his calling, and therefore, he is prepared to accept any risk, including death, in order to follow it. He is not a wilful martyr, but once he has said:

> Now is my way clear, now is the meaning plain:
> Temptation shall not come in this kind again.
> The last temptation is the greatest treason:
> To do the right deed for the wrong reason

—he will not turn again, he will fare forward, following not his will, but the will of God. He goes on to explain, in the Christmas sermon, that:

> "A Christian martyrdom is never an accident, for Saints are not made by accident. Still less is a Christian martyrdom the effect of a man's will to become a Saint, as a man by willing and contriving may become a ruler of men. A martyrdom is always the design of God, for His love of men, to warn them and to lead them, to bring them back to His ways. It is never the design of man; for the true martyr is he who has become the instrument of God, who has lost his will in the will of God, and who no longer desires anything for himself, not even the glory of being a martyr.

Therefore we are not watching a conflict of protagonists, passions or duties, but the unfolding of the will of God. The successive temptations, with the exception of the last, are easily disposed of, and even the last does not make it possible to know exactly what Becket's will truly is. We must accept it for what he declares it to be, perfect obedience to the will of God—something which is confirmed by the Christmas sermon.

The chorus mirrors the hesitations of Becket's mind; they "know and do not know". The women of the chorus are neither ignorant nor blind, and their plight, which Becket's spiritual ascent accentuates, is very moving:

> We are not ignorant women, we know what we must
>                    expect and not expect.
>
> . . .
> And meanwhile we have gone on living,
> Living and partly living,
> Picking together the pieces,
> Gathering faggots at nightfall,
> Building a partial shelter,
> For sleeping, and eating and drinking and laughter.

They accept their share in the "eternal burden, the perpetual glory", which are the burden of sin and the glory of redemption, and their humanity suffuses the play and gives it a human dimension which Becket's sense of vocation precludes:

> Human kind cannot bear very much reality.
>
> . . .
>
> All my life they have been coming, these feet. All my life
> I have waited. Death will come only when I am worthy,
> And if I am worthy, there is no danger.
> I have therefore only to make perfect my will.

The action of the play is neither carried out by the main character nor does it grow linearly in time; it is a cumulative form of action, or—should one rather say—a progressive dawning of light or illumination which enforces upon Becket the significance and necessity of his death, and upon the audience the moving wisdom that truth and the unfolding of the historical process cannot take place without the dire exaction of blood and tears. These are views prompted by the contemplation of the play as an intrinsic entity and which therefore do not allow the dramatic weaknesses, most of them detected by the author himself, to detract substantially from the very high level of achievement. One has only to compare it with the other Beckets, by Tennyson, Anouilh or Fry, to realize that if Eliot cannot match Anouilh's dramatic skill, which is not needed in this case, the emotions with which he deals have a true Aristotelian nobility and purity, and the martyred figure of his archbishop is likely to keep all the other attempts at depicting him in the shade for a long time to come.

The verse of *Murder in the Cathedral* remains somehow a motley garb which has not been fully woven into a single texture. The chorus's presence naturally slows down the action, which, of course, is not the same type of action as that of *The Family Reunion*. There is here no dramatic suspense; the audience knows what will come next, in the same way as Greek audiences knew every move of the great plays which they witnessed. In a sense, *Murder in the Cathedral* is a ritual; it is the re-enactment of a redeeming death; yet this does not fully dispose of the fact that a certain amount of the verse is either mono-voiced or static, and that it acts as a kind of commentary to the action. The audiences know very clearly that they are listening to verse, and generally they like it, for the audiences which love religious plays are special audiences conditioned to ritual, hieratic speech and noble style. But Eliot wanted an audience who would neither look upon poetry as something unnatural nor feel that it had to put on its special poetic soul whenever it was going to listen to a poetic play. Verse had therefore to be made as natural as possible, and transition between verse and prose or between different types of verse had to be avoided as being bewildering and as preventing the audience from giving itself unselfconsciously to the flow of the dramatic action. "We should aim at a form of verse in which everything can be said that has to be said; and . . . when we find some situation which is intractable in verse, it is merely that our form of verse is inelastic. And if there prove to be scenes which we cannot put in verse, we must either develop our verse, or avoid having to introduce such scenes. For we have to accustom our audiences to verse to the point at which they will cease to be conscious of it; and to introduce prose dialogue, would only be to distract their attention from the play itself to the medium of its expression. But if our verse is to have so wide a range that it can say anything that has to be said, it follows that it will not be 'poetry' all the time. It will only be 'poetry' when the dramatic situation has reached such a point of intensity that poetry becomes the natural utterance, because then it is the only language in which the emotions can be expressed at all." (*Selected Prose*, p. 70.)

For his next play, Eliot was determined to choose a contemporary theme and to evolve a form of verse close to contemporary speech. The result was *The Family Reunion*. The basic or the essential search was not very different from that of *Murder in the Cathedral*. It was the search for purity and holiness, and it is a search which will be continued in various forms in *The Cocktail Party* and in the plays which followed. It is in fact man's most fundamental search, his search for the essential truth which will enable him to close his eyes with the words:

"la sua volontate è nostra pace". The prop of the historical subject having been discarded, Eliot replaced it by the prop of a Greek myth which, from now on, will be the infra-structure of his themes which are both modern and perennial. That of *The Family Reunion* comes from *The Oresteia* and more particularly from *The Choephoroi* and *The Eumenides*. Harry is a kind of Orestes who, instead of having killed his mother, may have killed his wife; at any rate he has the feeling that he may have done so.

Why? Well, as Sweeney in *Sweeney Agonistes* said, "any man might do a girl in, any man . . . wants to . . ."; besides, his father had certainly wanted to kill his mother, and Harry carries with him the guilt of his ancestry. He is therefore anything but the plain scion of a well-to-do family; he is a symbolic character, a kind of Hamlet at odds with his world. He is everyman in search of purity. He could be cured by psychoanalysis or by faith. The aunts and uncles are also at least as ambivalent as he is; they are what they are, and they are, at the same time, the commenting chorus. There are also the Eumenides, who have to be placated by penance and acceptance of guilt, and turned into friendly divinities; and as such, they have given endless trouble to their author and to various producers who have directed the play. Then, there are the chauffeur, the police inspector and Harry's simpleton of a brother. We have altogether a naturalistic setting, a veneer of naturalism for the characters, and we have everywhere the lurking shadows of a symbolic world which carries the action deep down into the past and far and wide beyond the social context to which these characters belong. This is an extremely subtle use of mythical and referential terms in order to lift the action out of the present and out of naturalism into the world of imagination and poetry.

A brief comparison between the Greek play, on which Eliot has based his story and theme, and the modern version which he has given of them, shows that it has not been possible to fuse the two stories and themes together into a perfect dramatic unity. The failure to achieve this unity leaves the play with two slight flaws. One lies in the character of Harry, and the other in the use of the Eumenides. Eliot himself saw these two flaws much more clearly than anyone else, and has pointed them out: "They (the Eumenides) must, in future, . . . be understood to be visible only to certain of my characters, and not to the audience. We tried every possible manner of presenting them. We put them on the stage, and they looked like uninvited guests who had strayed in from a fancy-dress ball. We concealed them behind gauze, and they suggested a still out of a Walt Disney film. We made them dimmer, and they looked like shrubbery just outside the window. I have seen other expedients tried: I have seen them signalling from across the garden, or swarming on to the stage like a football team, and they are never right. They never succeed in being either Greek goddesses or modern spooks." (*Selected Prose*, p. 82.) This incapacity of the Eumenides to be either Greek—therefore integral parts of a religious world—or modern, is one of the weaknesses of the play. The other weakness concerns the character of Harry, about whom Eliot said, in a letter to Mr. Hugh Beaumont dated 4th July 1955: "I now find that the play is not so much the comedy of Harry Monchensey as the tragedy of his mother."

Eliot wanted to follow up *Murder in the Cathedral* with another Christian play, but this time set in modern society. Having these aims in view, he thought he could give depth to his play by using the infra-structure of a Greek play which dealt with the problem which preoccupied him—the problem of guilt and liberation from the depth of despair. Eliot neither wanted his play to be overtly Christian, something which would have classed it in the category of religious drama and therefore limited its appeal, nor explicitly supported by a Greek framework, a device which was alien to his natural discretion and love of allusiveness, and also to the fact that, being extremely learned, he proceeded by subtle hints and not by bold displays of knowledge. He forgot the fact that *The Oresteia* is not so well known as he probably thought, and that few are those who see the shadow of Orestes lurking behind Harry; yet, this shadow plays a very important part in the understanding of the latter's behaviour. To begin with, there is a curse upon the Monchenseys, as there was a curse on the house of the Atrides. This

curse has to be expiated by a member of the family, a scape-
goat for the family. Orestes kills his mother, who was guilty
of the murder of his father, is haunted by the Eumenides, and
finally absolved of his crime by a human tribunal in which
Pallas Athene takes part. So the Eumenides are placated and
they leave Orestes in peace.

The problem here is twofold: first, how to make these deities
of the Greek underworld tangible to a modern audience,
who no more believe in them than in the witches of *Macbeth*;
secondly, how to show their transformation from fury to
benevolence. The curse is obviously the curse of original sin, and
of man's necessity to be reborn in order to be rid of its weight.
In the Greek play, the Eumenides change; in Eliot's play, it is
Harry—Orestes—who changes, who is transformed by the same
inflexible laws, whether in England or in Argos. Harry must
know the true guilt of his family before he can know and
expiate his own. Like the Confidential Clerk, he must know who
his father was, and once he knows his past, he understands his
present and the future he must make for himself. The process
followed is therefore that of tragedy, which consists in a progressive dawning of the truth on the hero, who, once he realizes
the extent of his guilt, accepts death as rebirth. Once Harry has
been reborn, the Eumenides, though he still sees them, torment
him no more; yet he can no longer accept the life of the past.
He will not, like Celia or Becket, die the death of a martyr, but
he must get out of the world, undertake some mission in the
desert, so as to divest himself of "the love of created beings",
as St. John of the Cross says. This quotation from St. John of
the Cross is part of the epigraph of *Sweeney Agonistes*, the other
being an extract from *The Choephoroi*, when Orestes says:
"You don't see them, you don't—but *I* see them: they are
hunting me down, I must move on." Harry, at the end of his
most moving conversation with Mary, says just that, and there
is no doubt that the bonds between Sweeney and Harry are
real. The difference between the two is that Sweeney could yield
to the human temptation of "doing a girl in", while Harry is
too inhibited, too obsessed by his sense of sin, to actually perform such an act; he can only perform it mentally, just as did

his father before him, who, instead of murdering his unloved wife, left her to go and die in a distant place.

The play has a true classical purity. The action, entirely psychological, lasts only three hours, the exact duration of the play, which is also the time Harry spends at Wishwood where his "sick soul" finds the reasons for its sickness and the incentive to open its wings towards new horizons. When the play begins, eight years have elapsed since his departure and Harry returns to Wishwood, where the family is gathered to receive him and to celebrate his mother's birthday. His mother, Amy, has had one single purpose, which is to keep Wishwood alive so as to pass it on to Harry, who is obviously her favourite son:

> If you want to know why I never leave Wishwood
> That is the reason. I keep Wishwood alive
> To keep the family alive, to keep them together,
> To keep me alive, and I live to keep them.
> You none of you understand how old you are
> And death will come to you as a mild surprise,
> A momentary shudder in a vacant room.

There are two other sisters, Ivy and Agatha, who quickly remind Harry that "Wishwood has always been a cold place". There are uncles; there is a distant cousin of the family, Mary, and there are two other sons who are awaited. But what counts is Harry, who has made a marriage of convenience and whose wife has died mysteriously a year ago. Life at Wishwood is "living and partly living", and although the arrival of Harry is causing some expectancy, he is no saint, no Becket, to transform all that. In one way, he certainly transforms the scene, but not in the way expected by his mother. Harry no sooner arrives than he shouts:

> No, no, not there. Look there!
> Can't you see them? *You* don't see them, but I see them,
> And they see me. This is the first time that I have seen them.
> In the Java Straits, in the Sunda Sea,
> In the sweet sickly tropical night, I knew they were coming.

Of course nobody sees "them", and he stuns them all by describing his solitude, his suffering, his obsessions:

> The partial anaesthesia of suffering without feeling
> And partial observation of one's own automatism
> While the slow stain sinks deeper through the skin
> Tainting the flesh and discolouring the bone—
> This is what matters, but it is unspeakable,
> Untranslatable: I talk in general terms
> Because the particular has no language. One thinks to escape
> By violence, but one is still alone
> In an over-crowded desert, jostled by ghosts.
> It was only reversing the senseless direction
> For a momentary rest on the burning wheel
> That cloudless night in the mid-Atlantic
> When I pushed her over.

His mother prescribes a hot bath, after which he will, according to her, feel better. The questioning of Harry's chauffeur, Downing, by the uncles elicits some information about Harry's married life and therefore contributes to the knowledge of Harry's character. The scene with Mary is the most moving and the most lyrical of the play. The shared reminiscences of childhood reveal glimpses of lost innocence, symbolized by "the hollow tree in what we called the wilderness", and slowly rise to an admirable duet in which Mary's feminine sympathy and understanding seem to awaken possible glimmers of hope in Harry, who, for one moment, sings in unison with her, while his remorse-laden conscience is caught in a brief lull; and to Mary's words:

> Pain is the opposite of joy
> But joy is a kind of pain
> I believe the moment of birth
> Is when we have knowledge of death
> I believe the season of birth
> Is the season of sacrifice

—he answers:

Whether I know what I am saying, or why I say it,
That does not matter. You bring me news
Of a door that opens at the end of a corridor,
Sunlight and singing; when I had felt sure
That every corridor only led to another,
Or to a blank wall; that I kept moving
Only so as not to stay still. Singing and light.

Then, suddenly, in the middle of this vision of liberation, his conscience, the conscience of a merciless, sin-obsessed introverted person, who ceaselessly punishes himself for his own sins—imaginary or real—and for those of others, cannot allow this possibility of undeserved joy (since he thinks that, either physically or morally, he murdered his wife), intervenes and confronts him with the living remorse and fury of the Eumenides. This scene seems to me pervaded with deep psychological truth. Harry cannot allow himself to feel attracted physically and affectively by a woman, for he has loathed one woman to the point of wishing or perhaps even of causing her death, and this woman obviously recalls the other and his sin. He must first of all expiate this terrifying guilt. Mary, who has the quality of sympathy, sees the Eumenides as Harry sees them, but in order to help him, she pretends that she does not, and she draws the curtains. Harry thinks that she is imperceptive, like everybody else, while it is he who has not yet understood that in order to truly live, he must be reborn. Nevertheless, he has had a moment of illumination which will not be lost, for it will teach him that it is not at Wishwood that he will find his true reborn self. Agatha will complete the revelation which Mary has begun, and as these revelations can only lead to a shedding of human attachments, Mary, alas, one of the attractive characters of the play, will have to be left to go her own way in solitude:

We must all go, each in his own direction.
You, and I, and Harry. You and I,
My dear, may very likely meet again
In our wanderings in the neutral territory
Between two worlds.

Harry's curse, his original sin, is that he is not loved. He has been conceived in un-love; he is unloved by his mother, and he has neither loved nor been loved by his wife, whom he hated to the point of thinking of killing her, or of actually believing that he has killed her. He repeats his father's life. Mary is a young woman, capable of awakening physical desire, and with it, of course, in the case of Harry, immediate revulsion against such a feeling, which, for him, is associated with all the horror and loathing which married life with a woman whom he hated has caused him. So Mary has no chance of being accepted, or of being able to save him; but she has played her part, even if this has broken her heart. She has prepared the ground for Agatha, whose love is purely affective and who can act as the midwife or the psychiatrist to reveal to him his true past and the cause of his burden of guilt. The scene with Dr. Warburton, which precedes Agatha's intervention, only confirms Harry's callousness towards his mother. He simply does not care whether she lives or dies. It therefore shows the extent to which he is himself half-dead and in need of revival. This is the work of Agatha, and this she can do, because she herself has truly loved and suffered, and because, like Violaine in Claudel's famous play, she has a strong belief in spirit, so strong that, although she has not brought him into the world, she can look upon Harry as her own son, and the son of the man she truly loved and who loved her. This enables her to communicate with him and to reach him. Harry looks upon her as someone "liberated from the human wheel". He does not know that she had to fight for many years to win her dispossession. "Who are my parents?" says Harry and Agatha explains how, after his legal parents had spent three years learning together the meaning of loneliness, she joined them, and how the irremediable, or perhaps the predestined, happened. She and Harry's father recognized each other in an ineffable moment:

> There are hours when there seems to be no past or future,
> Only a present moment of pointed light
> When you want to burn. When you stretch out your hand
> To the flames. They only come once,
> Thank God, that kind. Perhaps there is another kind,
> I believe, across a whole Tibet of broken stones
> That lie, fang up, a lifetime's march. I have believed this.

She has known heaven and hell. We are back to *Burnt Norton*'s shaft of sunlight and glimpses of Dante's Hell of suffering. Harry begins to understand what his life could have been, and he even wonders if his actual life has not merely been a dream. But Agatha tells him that what she has told him is not a story of detection,

> Of crime and punishment, but of sin and expiation.
> It is possible that you have not known what sin
> You shall expiate, or whose, or why. It is certain
> That the knowledge of it must precede the expiation.
> It is possible that sin may strain and struggle
> In its dark instinctive birth, to come to consciousness
> And so find expurgation.

Harry, like Orestes, must take upon himself the curse of the family and go through purgatory. He understands, and he says:

> Look, I do not know why,
> I feel happy for a moment, as if I had come home.
> It is quite irrational, but now
> I feel quite happy, as if happiness
> Did not consist in getting what one wanted
> Or in getting rid of what can't be got rid of
> But in a different vision. This is like an end.

Agatha chimes in with the words, "And a beginning", and we are projected forwards to the "In my beginning is my end" of *East Coker*. Harry has seen the light, he has been wounded in a war of phantoms; he might, he says, become even fonder of his mother, and live in public, for he has got rid of the phantoms of convention and appearances, and he has recognized that his sense of guilt is real and that therefore he must meet his phantoms, however painful that may be, for this pain is also his freedom. Agatha answers with moving pathos in words which flow straight from *Burnt Norton*:

> I only looked through the little door
> When the sun was shining on the rose-garden:
> And heard in the distance tiny voices
> And then a black raven flew over.

131

And the two, using striking, direct, concentrated imagery, go on to explain their solitary suffering until they meet at last "in the rose-garden", which is for both the beginning of a new life. From now on, the Eumenides, instead of being Harry's shadowy pursuers—the expression of his guilt—become his guides which he will follow in order to achieve the salvation and liberation which Agatha foresees:

> O my child, my curse,
> You shall be fulfilled:
> The knot shall be unknotted
> And the crooked made straight.
> . . .        Love compels cruelty
> To those who do not understand love.
> What you have wished to know, what you have learned
> Mean the end of a relation, make it impossible.
> You did not intend this, I did not intend it,
> No one intended, but. . . . You must go.

And Harry, who feels that he must have been "elected" or chosen, goes, leaving his mother, who dies of heart failure.

So ends this extraordinary play, extraordinary by its complexity, and by the feelings which it prompts. It is obviously the work of a major poet, a profound thinker and a deeply religious man. Harry is one of the most complex characters of the modern stage, and I believe that only a good actor can bring to life or exteriorize the harrowing, terrifying forces which torment him and make him so uncompromising to himself and to others, until he discovers the cause of the terrors which tear his heart apart. He is obviously gnawed, eaten up by internal conflicts which are difficult to grasp from the outside. The Atrides' curse came from the gods whom they had disobeyed and outraged, and therefore they and their descendants had to expiate, through suffering, the wrongs which had been committed. All this was thoroughly understandable and acceptable to a society which believed in the immutable principles which ruled the lives of men as well as those of the gods. The curse of original sin, which may be said to apply to all mankind (for those who believe in it), cannot be particularized and concentrated on one single family; therefore, in as far as it is particular, the curse of the Monchensey family is simply due to the fact that Harry was born of a possessive, rather narrow-minded woman who neither truly loved, nor really missed true love, and who, when she lost the undisputed ownership of her husband's feelings, turned her possessiveness on her children and on Wishwood. Agatha seems to have been born to love Harry's father, who needed love. Agatha had both the intelligence and the capacity to love and to be loved that Amy lacked, but fate had decreed otherwise. So Harry was conceived in un-love, born from the wrong mother, doomed to be unloved, and he himself naturally married a woman whom he did not love, who did not love him, and whom he ended in hating. But the fact that Amy was not lovable is not, strictly speaking, a curse; it only makes of her a case for psychiatric treatment, and of her death a sad event, but not a tragedy.

Just as the curse of the Monchenseys, which at the particular level is not of religious origin, cannot be experienced in a modern society in the way in which the Greeks could experience and tremble at the fate of the Atrides pursued by gods in whom they believed, in the same way the Eumenides cannot play, in our time, a part which is purely a matter of individual conscience, and the pangs of individual conscience can only be exteriorized through actions or reactions. *The Family Reunion* follows the tragic pattern and is practically shorn of actions or events, except for the final death of Amy. This is the pattern of many of Chekhov's plays, which are the most moving of modern tragedies. *The Family Reunion* is a Chekhovian play, that is to say, a modern tragedy. However unlovable its main character may be, Harry's painful ascent towards the light is deeply human, moving, and the source of compassionate feelings. All in all, and bearing in mind the mastery of the form and the beauty of the poetry, this is undeniably a great play.

*The Cocktail Party* marks a definite progress in various aspects of the drama which Eliot was trying to bring to life. The dramatic skill has increased, the blend between Greek myth and modern situation has been perfected, the verse has been fully integrated. It hardly carries any traces of choral speech;

it still carries, when required—and it does so often enough—
a good deal of very moving poetry. It has become, by now, a
perfectly fluid and functional mode of expression. The different
voices are clearly differentiated and the verse moves from very
prosaic statements to poetry without faltering or attracting conscious attention to the transitions. The purple patches, the
moments of lyricism disconnected from drama, have been firmly
eliminated, and one has now a fluent, accurate and perfectly
confident dramatic medium.

In Euripides, Alcestis consents· to die in order to save her
husband's life, and Hercules, who is always in search of a good
deed, decides to bring her back·from the underworld. Alcestis
corresponds to both Lavinia and Celia, that is to say to two
aspects of femininity and to two levels of life in general. Lavinia
does not die to save her husband; she merely leaves him alone
so that he may find himself. When they both meet again after
their brief respective journeys, not through the desert but
through life, they have both learnt to avoid excessive expecta-
tions; they both know now that they do not understand each
other and that they must make the best of their humdrum
existences. Celia is the woman who sacrifices herself. She began,
like Lavinia, Edward and Peter Quilpe, by living in the dark,
in a world of blindness or partial blindness from which they all
have to move towards a form of light. But once Celia has been
touched by grace and has achieved a vision of the true life, she
can no longer accept compromise and humdrum existence, and
she becomes a pre-ordained martyr. Reilly is both Hercules and
Pheres; he is the quizzical, jolly fellow, full of drink and songs,
and he is the rescuer and healer who moves in an atmosphere
of mystery which grips the play from the very moment the cocktail party of the beginning draws to a close and Edward
remains alone with the strange, uninvited guest who seems no
ordinary man.

The listener clutches in vain at the naturalistic setting and
at the elements which first met his attention; he cannot help
becoming more and more unsettled and more and more aware
that things are anything but what they seem to be, and that he
is moving in an ambivalent world, which is liable to confront

him at any moment with profound and disturbing revelations. He soon discovers that the light-headed Mayfair socialite, Julia, who talks like seven and seems such an inconsequential woman, is in fact the leader of the action around her. She is endowed with strange powers which go further than Reilly's, and together with Alex, who seems at the beginning to be simply a gay dog about town, they are the "guardians", those who know and can guide others towards their salvation, either through humdrum existence or, for those who are called, through martyrdom. Celia's martyrdom is as much part of her destiny as Becket's:.

> So it was obvious
> That here was a woman under sentence of death.
> That was her destiny. The only question
> Then was, what sort of death? *I* could not know;
> Because it was for her to choose the way of life
> To lead to death, and, without knowing the end
> Yet choose the form of death. We know the death she chose.
> I did not know that she would die in this way,
> *She* did not know. So all that I could do
> Was to direct her in the way of preparation.

Although the death of Celia could have been less colourful, the religious theme of the play emerges steadily and ripples out, embracing all the aspects of the social life to which the characters belong, and carrying with it an aura of greater and greater light, which lifts the "comedy" to a high level of dramatic achievement.

In *The Cocktail Party*, as well as in *Alcestis*, a marriage has ended, and it must be made to begin again. Yet, the resemblances are only very superficial, and merely a means to give depth to a modern comedy. Harcourt-Reilly, like Hercules, appears at first as a badly behaved guest, and like Hercules, but for different reasons, he asks Lavinia to return to her husband, not veiled, as is the case in *Alcestis*, but as a total stranger, which is in fact the same thing. In order to attempt a fresh start, there must be no questions asked. *The Cocktail Party* is about the breakdown of a marriage, and para-religious means are used in order to mend it, or to make the best of a bad job. The structure of the play is in perfect conformity with that of high comedy. There is not only the husband and wife, Edward and Lavinia Chamberlayne, there is also a couple of younger people: Celia Coplestone, who has been Edward's mistress, and Peter Quilpe, who has been Lavinia's lover, but who has fallen in love with Celia. Besides Harcourt-Reilly as Hercules-psychiatrist, there are two people who act as his assistants: an elderly lady, Mrs. Julia Shuttlethwaite, the perfect socialite, a type which Eliot has used over and over again, and a young man, Alex MacColgie Gibbs, who, though he has no winged feet, behaves as a modern Mercury who knows and sees everything. These two are what are called the "guardians"—angels, shepherds, what one likes.

Just as in the Greek world of Euripides, these modern characters of comedy seem to be entirely free from the ups and downs of living, working and social pressures. True, Peter is a film-maker, and Harcourt-Reilly is some kind of mysterious psychiatrist, but they all have for the moment only one problem to solve, that of finding, if possible, some form of happiness, on earth or in heaven. The play is about the search for and the discovery of what one truly is, and about the various ways of coming to terms with such discoveries. Edward Chamberlayne thought he was a passionate lover; so he finds it difficult to square such an illusion with the unwelcome fact revealed to him by his former lover, Celia, who describes him thus:

> I think—I believe—you are being yourself
> As you never were before, with me.
> Twice you have changed since I have been looking at you.
> I looked at your face: and I thought that I knew
> And loved every contour; and as I looked
> It withered, as if I had unwrapped a mummy.
> I listened to your voice, that had always thrilled me,
> And it became another voice—no, not a voice:
> What I heard was only the noise of an insect.
> Dry, endless, meaningless, inhuman—
> You might have made it by scraping your legs together . . .

He is only:

> what was left
> Of what I had thought you were. I see another person,
> I see you as a person whom I never saw before.
> The man I saw before, he was only a projection—
> I see that now—of something that I wanted—
> No, not *wanted*—something I aspired to—
> Something that I desperately wanted to exist.

She has only known appearances—a name, a voice, and mannerisms, which she has transformed according to her needs. This is pure Bradley, but also pure human truth. Edward is, in fact, an egoist who can only think of himself, and his wife Lavinia is an ambitious and vain woman; therefore she is perfectly suited to him. They both need love as a prop or as a compensation. Edward needs to be loved to satisfy his ego, and Lavinia needs to love or to pretend to love to satisfy her own needs:

> You had wanted to be loved;
> You had come to see that no one had ever loved you.
> Then you began to fear that no one *could* love you.
> . . .
> And now you begin to see, I hope,
> How much you have in common. The same isolation.
> A man who finds himself incapable of loving
> And a woman who finds that no man can love her.

Celia is made of different stuff; she is truly absolute for love, and this absoluteness terrifies Edward, who cannot understand absolutes. Total devotion demands total response, and this kind of equilibrium is difficult to find and to maintain. Those who are born with such a need in their hearts cannot compromise; they must find it or die, for death for them is life:

> I have thought at moments that the ecstasy is real
> Although those who experience it may have no reality.
> For what happened is remembered like a dream
> In which one is exalted by intensity of loving
> In the spirit, a vibration of delight
> Without desire, for desire is fulfilled
> In the delight of loving. A state one does not know
> When awake. But what, or whom I loved,
> Or what in me was loving, I do not know.

F

Peter, who is all in the world, and intent upon world success, cannot satisfy her, though his brief encounter with the kind of meteorite that she is will for ever illuminate his life and give him a glimmer of the dream world which he will never have access to. Yet he will never forget that life is not all as he sees it, and that there is another crown more important than the crown of success.

The "guardians" provide the comic elements of the plot, and they help the various characters to cooperate with Reilly in order to discover the truth about themselves, or rather the truth which is in themselves, that is to say the voice, more or less strong, of their conscience. The crux of the play lies in the distinction between absolute love and average tenderness, kindness and forgiveness between persons who can share their solitariness, without dreaming of or desiring ecstatic unions, which are rather rare in life and can only be reached, by those who are intent upon it, through a death which is also a rebirth.

The next play, *The Confidential Clerk*, marks the completion of Eliot's search for a perfect blend of dramatic form with characters and action. The title itself—the "confidential clerk" and not the "private secretary"—is a way of distancing the play from naturalism and from the present. He has gone again to Euripides, to *Ion*, for the infra-structure of the action. The two worlds which are part of Eliot's thought are, this time, much better blended than in any other of his plays, since they are close enough to form, at times, one, and since the play is primarily a comedy with very serious undertones. The two worlds are the world of commerce and the world of art. Art is more accessible than religion, and though it has had its monks and its martyrs, it neither requires the asceticism and sacrifices of religion, nor can it offer the same type of beatitude. So Colby, who corresponds to Celia, will not die at the end of the play, but having discovered his true origins, and therefore having reached the stage of knowing himself, he will practise the art which he loves, and he may even enter religion, for he is a highly religious man. Before the final discovery of his vocation, music was for him a kind of religion, in the same way as ceramics and spiritualism were the private religions of Sir

Claude and his wife. But there are no substitutes for religion, and those who lack faith or who try to replace it by something else can only lead fragmented existences, without a centre. Colby and the Mulhammers have their private gardens which they enter every now and then, but only Eggerson, who is a religious man, lives in an integrated world in which his garden is fruitful and is truly part of his life. Sir Claude and Colby realize that they lack the creative gift that they have longed for or thought they had, and, having discovered the truth about their origins and about their parents, they come to terms with life, and decide each to follow the path which is marked for him. The tension of the play is lower than that of *The Cocktail Party*, but the blend of the various planes is more successful. The verse has been pruned, chastened still more, and it offers no opportunity for elevated poetic speech. Even the most moving encounters between Colby and Sir Claude, and Colby and Lucasta, are so restrained, so controlled, that the actors could not attempt to raise their voices and speak the lines as obvious verse, without getting out of character.

Colby and Lucasta are not meant to be tempestuous, passionate or star-crossed lovers; they are everyday human beings, caught in the grip of situations in which they struggle without shrieks or gestures, because that is not their nature; yet they are not less moving for that. They are no Cuchulain or Deirdre of the Sorrows, and their subdued speech has the spare greyness of a world of cement and stones with, here and there, a patch of green. Of course, most of what they say could have been said in prose, but who could have said it? Only Eliot himself, for no other dramatist has yet succeeded in blending such a sophisticated type of comedy with the religious seriousness which is part of his great gifts. Anouilh can be both comic and serious, but the two levels are never held together or projected through a highly sophisticated and, at the same time, deeply religious sensibility. The listener or reader is here given the facts, which the author has transmuted into an entity which imposes its own terms. To refuse these terms, to say that *The Confidential Clerk* could have been written in prose or that it could have carried more poetry, is to ask for something very different from what the author tried to do or would have been willing to do. The kind of poetry which some poetry-lovers would wish to see on the stage cannot be associated with themes like that of *The Confidential Clerk* or *The Elder Statesman*. It could only be associated with heroic or emotion-laden themes, with highly individualized and partially symbolic characters, which require another poet-playwright and, above all, another public.

The theme of *The Confidential Clerk* could be: "know who your parents are, and in knowing that you will be able to choose your true vocation". "Who was your father?" is a typical theme of comedy, but the choices which follow such searches are, for Eliot, something profound and serious, for they are bound to reach, in certain cases, the metaphysical plane. The play starts with a criss-crossing of hidden identities which obviously appealed to a Sherlock Holmes reader like Eliot. Mrs. Guzzard (and what a name!) decided long ago that her son Colby would pass as her sister's son, and not as her own, because, her sister being Sir Claude Mulhammer's mistress, Colby would have a better chance in life as the supposed son of the rich Sir Claude than as the son of Mrs. Guzzard and her late organist husband. Her sister was expecting a child from Sir Claude, who was, at the time, in Canada. Lady Mulhammer has had an illegitimate son which she has given to a foster mother, whose name she has forgotten. Sir Claude himself has an illegitimate daughter, Lucasta, who is passed off as the daughter of a friend. He has also chosen to act as Colby's patron and not as his father, which, in fact, he is not. His passion is pottery. Colby's passion is music, but Sir Claude tries to dissuade him from cultivating this passion, saying that he will never be anything else but a second-rate musician, and that therefore he had better concentrate on his job.

Colby Simpkins is everyone's dream. Everyone wants him as the ideal son or husband, until the truth is revealed. This is done by the Mme. Sosostris of Teddington, his would-be Aunt Sarah Guzzard, who is really his mother. The truth is that Colby's father was an unsuccessful organist, and on hearing this Colby declares that he will go the way of his true father; he will work as an organist in the church of Joshua Park, and live with Sir Claude's old clerk, Eggerson. Eggerson is the only person in the play who is fully at peace with himself and with his surroundings. He is also, like Alex or Julia in *The Cocktail Party*, a kind of guardian. He is a true father and a true husband. He has brought up and lost a son, whom Colby will replace, and he has a true relationship with nature; his garden is not an escape or a dream, it is a true garden, and as such, he can reach in it states of perfect communion, which necessarily link him with the notion of dream garden which we find time and again in Eliot's poetry as a symbol of moments of bliss and timelessness. Colby will bring contentment to the Eggerson household, and without getting out of the world, like Celia, in *The Cocktail Party*, he might nevertheless fulfil his destiny and vocation by taking holy orders and working for his Heavenly Father.

Sir Claude is left with his wife in practically the same way as Edward Chamberlayne was left with his. He will have to make the best he can of a situation in which everyone's true nature has been laid bare. He will have to give an allowance to his not much loved daughter, who will marry Lady Elizabeth's newly discovered extremely vulgar offspring, Barnabas Kaghan. Lady Elizabeth will have to accept her husband's mediocrity and fake artistic longings, and put an end to a merry-go-round of make-believe. Everyone will have to stick to what he truly is, and fulfil willy-nilly his true vocation, which he sought to disguise under wishful thinking and social attitudinizing.

With *The Elder Statesman*, Eliot returns to a theme of guilt, akin to that of *The Family Reunion*. The difference is that here there has been no death, only two bad actions which weigh heavily on Lord Claverton's last days. He is an Ibsenian character, haunted by his past, which is alive in the shape of his ex-fellow student, Gomez, and his ex-sweetheart, Mrs. Carghill, who is related to Lady Mulhammer and, in certain respects, to Julia. Eliot has gone again to the Greeks for his scaffolding; this time he has made use of the *Oedipus Coloneus* of Sophocles. Lord Claverton with Monica-Antigone-Marina is on the way to the sacred grove where, purged of his guilt, he will die. His son Michael, who has been caught in the web of his sense of guilt, is Polynices, and also Harry of *The Family Reunion*. Lord Claverton needs no Tiresias to reveal to him the truth of his guilt; he knows it himself, he knows it perhaps with a rather disproportionate sense of its importance, for it is at all moments difficult to cast the same severity as he does upon the minor failings of his youth. One could say that he is in need of self-mortification, but that only underscores his humanity and his humility. He is no prig, like his distant relation Harry Monchensey; he does not try to be a saint or to blame anyone for his failings; he only blames himself, even if he overstresses the blame. He is therefore very human; we look upon him as "mon semblable, mon frère", leaving out the "hypocrite", which he is not. He is too clear-sighted for that and too intent on his moral responsibilities, including those towards his son. He obviously would like to love and to be loved, and it is his love for his daughter which impels his confession and contrition. For the first time in Eliot's theatre love between two young people comes to fruition and is presented as a normal manifestation of existence.

The characterization in this play is more marked than in any of the other plays, with the exception of Lord Claverton, who is given extra-naturalistic dimensions which prepare the ground for his noble death; the other characters are, each with his respective traits, recognizably human. Gomez, Mrs. Carghill, Mrs. Piggott, the butler, are straight out of everyday life, and Charles and Monica close the play with the kind of moving love duet which neither Celia and Peter Quilpe, nor Colby and Lucasta had been able to sing, and which bears the imprint of Eliot's newly found, long awaited happiness. The play is bathed in an atmosphere of graceful mellowness, quaint wit and benignity which bespeaks arrivals after tempests and peace in quiet coves or sacred woods.

The excessive scruples of Lord Claverton are both difficult to understand and ungrounded. The blackmailer who pursues him has not, in fact, been ruined by him, and the "secrets" which he purports to hold could not cause any scandal or stain

Lord Claverton's reputation. He could safely ignore Gomez as well as Mrs. Carghill's attempt to have a hold on him. They have both done extremely well out of life, and the past failures for which they blame Lord Claverton were above all their own; they know it, and they want to continue to cling to him as before. If he were not obsessed by his scruples, he would have rejected these eleventh-hour tempters, with as much alacrity as Becket displayed with his first three tempters. But he is as much haunted by his past as his blackmailers, and it is only once he has resolved to accept his past, and death, that he can be free of them:

> I've been freed from the self that pretends to be someone;
> And in becoming no one, I begin to live.
> It is worth while dying, to find out what life is.
> And I love you, my daughter, the more truly for knowing
> That there is someone you love more than your father—
> That you love and are loved. And now that I love Michael,
> I think, for the first time—remember, my dear,
> I am only a beginner in the practice of loving—
> Well, that is something.

Eliot's dramatic work is now out of fashion, with the exception of *Murder in the Cathedral* which continues to be acted, particularly in Europe, and to enjoy great success. Whatever the fashion of the moment may be, Eliot has certainly achieved the aim he had set himself, which was to create a form of "heightened speech" capable of passing without transition from poetry to prose, and making it possible to deal with themes of modern, everyday life, in terms of tragedy, as in *The Family Reunion*, or high comedy, as in *The Cocktail Party* and *The Confidential Clerk*. This body of work will live, and is very much alive now, for if there are no *Cocktail Parties*, there are *Birthday Parties* and *Tea Parties*, *Waiting* in Waste Lands, and various descendants of *Sweeney Agonistes*; so its author is assured of a lasting place among the great dramatists of the world.

# VIII

## CONCLUSION

Eliot was a very religious man, and as such, he was truly tolerant of all religions which imply spirituality and respect for life. Far from him the fierce dogmatism of a devout man like Claudel, who felt that the unbelievers, from Gide to Renan and Voltaire, should be confined to some kind of hell. Being a very religious man, his vision of the world was unified, and he was fully aware that men, irrespective of the place and time when they lived, had common aspirations and longings. His profound studies of Eastern and Western thought had made him aware of their complementariness, and of the need for the interpenetration and for a kind of synthesis of the two. Although Heaven and Nirvana are slightly different notions, the notion of reaching perfection through suffering and the shedding off of all earthly impediments—such as desires, ambitions and the demands of the senses—is common to both Christian and Hindu thought. The way of St. John of the Cross is also the way of the Hindu mystics, and though the figure which is at the summit of the Christian theogony is not the no-Being of Buddhism, the ascent towards it is similar, and, in the case of the mystics, it can be made along the same stairs. There is, of course, one fundamental difference between the two creeds, and it is summed up in Eliot's striking line: "Only through time time is conquered". In Christianity, time and eternity are not dissociated, they are inextricably linked, and one is the midwife of the other. Not so in Hinduism, in which Time and the body do not matter; what matters is to escape for ever from the wheel of Time.

The journey from barren time, time without faith, therefore time separated from transcendence, to Time redeemed by the Hanged Man, is the journey of Eliot's poetry and drama. The

144

speaking *I* of *The Waste Land* is also the Fisher King, the vegetation god who must die in order to be reborn. At this stage the good news of Christ's coming has not yet reached mankind, and His message and import can only be apprehended through primitive cults, or magic interventions, like that of the thunder at the end of the poem. After the deep despair of *The Hollow Men*, the despair which is the darkest moment before the dawn, or, as Dostoievsky put it, the despair of the one "who stands on the last rung but one before the attainment of the most perfect faith", Eliot ascends from the extremely moving depth through which his questing, light-obsessed soul has passed, to the heights and sun-blessed regions of *Ash Wednesday*. The music of the verse transmits the exaltation and ineffable joy of the liberated spirit, and from then on, through Shakespearian *Marina, A Song for Simeon* and *Journey of the Magi*, we move to the timelessness of vision of the *Quartets*, to the point where:

> Love is itself unmoving,
> Only the cause and end of movement . . .
> *(Burnt Norton)*

This timelessness is reached through love, which transcends itself beyond past and future:

> This is the use of memory:
> For liberation—not less of love but expanding
> Of love beyond desire, and so liberation
> From the future as well as the past.
> *(Little Gidding)*

In this vision of timelessness, which fuses Plato's love with the eternal rose of Dante's Heaven, there is even room for Krishna's wisdom:

> I sometimes wonder if that is what Krishna meant—
> Among other things—or one way of putting the same thing . . .
> *(The Dry Salvages)*

And there is also room for Hegelian dialectics and for Hegel's insistence that the incarnation is the absolute crux of Christianity, the true intersection of Time with timelessness.

## T. S. Eliot, Poet and Dramatist

From the moment Eliot reached the solid ground of his faith, no writer did more than he for the adaptation of Christianity to the needs of our time. Rejecting the label of Christian poet or Christian writer, which is too circumscribing for the scope of his interests, he allowed his artistic genius to be permeated by his deeply held religious convictions, and to transmute these convictions into works of art which are accessible to all those who, irrespective of the beliefs which they hold, can feel, through the perfections of his artistic syntheses, the impact of his Franciscan type of Christianity. *Murder in the Cathedral* is a religious play commissioned by a church to be originally acted in a church, yet, in spite of all that, and in spite of his theme which is that of martyrdom, the artistry and deep humanity of the work can be enjoyed and apprehended, even by those who do not share Becket's beliefs, because, whatever weaknesses the play may have, it is not didactic; it allows the central character and those who surround him to be themselves, and not the mouthpiece of the author.

The absence of the author, of the speaking *I*, is felt even more in the *Quartets*, in which, in spite of the concrete passages which relate each poem to reality and to moments of the poet's life, the overall experience which emanates from them is that of a vision held together by a mind or a prism suspended between heaven and earth, and which connects one with the other, while belonging to neither. One marvels at the way this vision has been captured, and one cannot help being transformed and ennobled by the awareness that a fellow human being could have been allowed to explore such distant spaces. The extraordinary musings of *La Jeune Parque*, oscillating between being and non-being, the heart-rending poignancy of the later poetry of Yeats, the Yeats of *Among School Children*, the Yeats of the *Byzantium* poems, *Purgatory* and *Crazy Jane*, the Yeats of:

> You think it horrible that lust and rage
> Should dance attendance upon my old age;
> They were not such a plague when I was young,
> What else have I to spur me into song?

or:

## Conclusion

I must lie down where all the ladders start
In the foul rag and bone shop of the heart.

—belong to the same world. These two types of experience suggested by the poetry of Valéry and Yeats, though different in many ways, partake in the end of the same existential preoccupations, and produce in us the same sense of awe and compassion for the nobility of man as with *Four Quartets*. Eliot, Yeats, and Valéry are, to my mind, the three summits of contemporary poetry, though, if one linked poetry with drama, as one ought to, then Claudel would have to be brought in.

Although Eliot, in his famous encomium at the grave of Yeats in 1940, handsomely implied that Yeats could be the greatest poet of his time—and I am inclined to believe that he may have been justified in doing so, particularly in as far as English literature is concerned—it seems to me evident that, all in all, Eliot is the most important and the most significant poet and critic of our time. I use these two terms advisedly, for they not only imply a certain level of greatness but, above all, they directly relate the poet to the society and the time in which he has lived; and in that respect no modern writer—poet, dramatist or novelist—can claim to have fulfilled his task better than Eliot.

As a critic, Eliot must take his place, a place apart beside the poet-critics like Dr. Johnson, Coleridge, Baudelaire and, on a lower scale, Matthew Arnold. It is not my purpose to discuss Eliot as a critic, for such a discussion should be the object of a special study implementing the requisite qualifications it would imply. It is sufficient to note here that his practically total reexamination of English literature has had deep repercussions and has contributed more than any other influence to the creation of a new artistic sensibility and to a revaluation of its major aspects. His reassessments of the Elizabethan and Jacobean dramatists, of Dante and of the metaphysical poets, of Milton and the great Romantics, have thrown new light on literature, and whether approved or disapproved of, they have stimulated great interest. His view of the creative process, his insistence on a unified sensibility, on an homogeneous society, on a sense

147

of tradition and history, and on impersonality, which he summed up with the words: ". . . the more perfect the artist, the more completely separate in him will be the man who suffers and the mind which creates" (*Selected Essays*, p. 18), together with his great concern for the renewal of the language of poetry, have had quite an influence on modern literature.

As a critic, I therefore think that he must take his place beside Baudelaire and Coleridge. As a poet, Eliot did not concern himself with trying to evolve new philosophical theories. He said explicitly enough in his essay on Dante that Dante was not an original thinker; that was not his task, and that he merely made use of the thought of his time. Eliot's view that "the great poet, in writing himself, writes his time", and that the essential function of the poet is "to express the greatest emotional intensity of his time, based on whatever his time happened to think" (*Selected Prose*, p. 55), echoes Hegel's view that the philosopher can no more get out of his time than one can get out of one's skin. Eliot certainly expresses his time, the time of Bergson, Jung, Freud, Frazer, of anthropological studies, mysticism, psychology and experiments in the arts, from cubism and surrealism to post-symbolistic, Proustian and Joycean impressionism and allusiveness in literature.

As for politics, although he has been at times maligned, he never was a rabid political animal. He disliked both anarchy and demagogy, and his inclinations were more towards élitism than equalitarianism. He believed, as he stated in *Little Gidding*, that in death opponents are folded in the same party, and he believed, above all, that life is community life:

> What life have you if you have not life together?
> There is no life that is not in community,
> And no community not lived in praise of GOD.
> *(The Rock)*

This search for an homogeneous type of community life implied for him a unity of cultural background and religion without which a society was not homogeneous. Looking at facts in the light of his sociological beliefs, he would have felt that an enclave of Moslems or of non-Christians in a Christian society would prevent homogeneity and preclude some kind of national consciousness. This has nothing to do with a kind of much decried nationalism which should be called purely and simply racialism—something which Eliot disliked intensely, as he disliked dictators, whether military, political or economic. Like thinkers as different as Hegel, Marx and Martin Buber, he believed that what matters is not the individual in isolation, but the individual in relation to other individuals, as part of a living, spiritually centred community. Thence his condemnation of mechanical sex, outside the context of true love, which must not be its own end and justification, but part of a higher, God-mediated love which embraces all men in a single brotherhood. That is why he disliked the fierce, egotistical individualism of the Romantics. "What is disastrous is that the writer should deliberately give rein to his 'individuality', that he should even cultivate his differences from others; and that his readers should cherish the author of genius, not in spite of his deviations from the inherited wisdom of the race, but because of them." (*After Strange Gods*, Faber, 1934, p. 33.) He was a Christian realist, looking upon the individual as part of a society with a past, of which one must be constantly aware, a present, and a future which, for Eliot, was informed with God's purpose. That is why he disliked materialism, behaviourism, utilitarianism, pragmatism and particularly scientific humanism—which he deplored, and about which he explained his views in the course of his criticism of Matthew Arnold, in *The Use of Poetry*.

The Arnoldean notion that art and religion are interchangeable, and that poetry is, at bottom, a criticism of life, is untenable. Eliot could not conceive of poetry as being reduced to such a mundane and superficial function; even less could he conceive of art, or humanism, as alternatives or substitutes for religion. At the bottom of life there must be, according to Eliot, a deeply held faith, a Pascalian sense of the contrast of the two infinites, a sense of both the horror and the glory of life, and an awareness of the terror of infinite spaces, impossible to face without some guiding hand or light. Eliot shared with Baudelaire, Dostoievsky and, to a large extent, Yeats, a religious attitude towards suffering, which refines and purifies. In our time,

Simone Weil held the same views. Without such beliefs, life is a Waste Land. Eliot, who, through the despair of his early life, was in a state of at-tention, heard the call and joined the Church of England in 1927. In doing so, he chose neither the church of his great hero, Dante, nor the church of his Puritan ancestor, whose indelible mark never left him, but the middle way—the Greek way, or the way of Buddha, the way of no extremes, which is represented by the Anglican High Church, in religion, in politics, or in life. His uncompromising individualism, which kept him away from social coteries and literary cliques, was tempered by his great faith in tradition and in the importance of the past, just as his idealism was tempered by and came to terms with his catholic taste. Whenever he yielded, as everyone does, to judgments influenced by times and circumstances, such as youthfulness and the desire to defend his own type of writing, he never hesitated to make amends, to recant, and humbly retrace his steps. He began by considering Goethe as a rather secondary writer; he ended in placing him by the side of Dante and Shakespeare. He deplored Shelley's lack of intellectual power; he paid homage to him in putting *The Triumph of Life* side by side with passages from Dante. He began by decrying Milton's influence; he ended in making amends for his rash views. The explanation is that "our sensibility is constantly changing, as the world about us changes: ours is not the same as that of the Chinese or the Hindu, but also it is not the same as that of our ancestors several hundred years ago. It is not the same as that of our fathers; and finally, we ourselves are not quite the same persons that we were a year ago." (*On Poetry and Poets*, p. 20.)

So much for changes of opinion due to changes in sensibility. Eliot has explained in various essays what he meant by poetry, and without labouring the point, it seems to me that one or two quotations from his essay on *The Social Function of Poetry* dispose of some misunderstandings and make clear his attitude. First of all the problem of the need for an homogeneous community, to which I have already alluded: "It is enough that in an homogeneous people the feelings of the most refined and complex have something in common with those of the most crude and simple, which they have not in common with those of people of their own level speaking another language. And, when a civilization is healthy, the great poet will have something to say to his fellow countrymen at every level of education." (*Idem*, p. 20.) Secondly, the problem of the audience of the poet: "Bad verse may have a transient vogue when the poet is reflecting a popular attitude of the moment; but real poetry survives not only a change of popular opinion but the complete extinction of interest in the issues with which the poet was passionately concerned. Lucretius' poem remains a great poem, though his notions of physics and astronomy are discredited. . . ." (*Idem*, pp. 17–18.) This is completed by a passage which describes exactly the part that Eliot has played in contemporary society: "There should always be a small vanguard of people, appreciative of poetry, who are independent and somewhat in advance of their time or ready to assimilate novelty more quickly. The development of culture does not mean bringing everybody up to the front, which amounts to no more than making everyone keep step: it means the maintenance of such an élite, with the main, and more passive body of readers not lagging more than a generation or so behind. The changes and developments of sensibility which appear first in a few will work themselves into the language gradually, through their influence on other, and more readily popular authors; and by the time they have become well established, a new advance will be called for." (*Idem*, p. 21.) Now, the changes in sensibility which he expressed have been partly absorbed and partly rejected by social developments which have moved further and further away from the values which Eliot upheld.

The notion of an élite, whatever its form or occupation, is anathema to our equalitarian society. Everybody is as good as anybody else, and everyone, from the painter of tin cans to the logorrhea-afflicted writer of doggerel and pop songs, is a poet, and the bigger his audience, the greater his worth. This worth is, of course, measured by his bank account. The mass media of communication, which operate simultaneously and on a world-wide level, have spread the notion that art must be accessible to everyone and at once. Raphael is the only one who, in the past, is supposed to have said: "I too am a painter". Now, every daub-splasher is a painter, every photographer, every instigator of a happening or of instantaneous theatre, is a creative artist. Tradition and the awareness of the past which Eliot found necessary in order to understand the present and to be truly contemporary, are despised and rejected, on the ground that they are impediments for coping with and understanding the present. All that matters now is doing, and cultivating one's own sensations, in a climate of world-wide provincialism.

Eliot never believed, like Sartre, that the poet or the writer could best contribute to social changes through direct action, on the barricades and in the streets, though he never shunned action when required, as in defence of Ezra Pound or of writers beyond the Iron Curtain. But he believed that every individual could best perform his social function by discovering and sticking to his true vocation, and by working within the medium which conforms with his talents or genius. He would not have confined himself to the famous "Ne sutor ultra crepida", but he never shared the ambitions of D'Annunzio, or those of a revolutionary hero like Che Guevara. I am sure he would have admired the latter's devotion to the betterment of the destitute, as he profoundly admired the saintly Simone Weil, but he would not have tried to emulate him in performing tasks for which he did not feel equipped. He was opposed to tyranny and to Communism in as far as Communism ignores the rights and sacredness of the human person and the vital importance of the spirit, but he recognized the heretical and, in many ways, Christian aspects of Marxism, in as far as it advocated the kind of brotherhood and love of men which are part of the Sermon on the Mount. His deep sense of human inadequacy without God and without grace was enhanced by a profound concern with history and time, which are also part of Marxism. He abhorred the authoritarianism and ruthlessness of Communism, but his deep Christian feelings involved him in history as a living, transforming force, which is continuously being transformed and made by men. His Christianity was active and involved in political life, and his individualism would undeniably have been on the side of all those who feel oppressed by the rigid, anonymous authority of the state, or of any sinister, Orwellian big brothers who rule by remote control and turn the artist into an entertainer or a clown, and the masses into amorphous material which can be shaped according to the will and purpose of the rulers. The despair of *The Waste Land* is still part of the contemporary world, uncertain of its future and without any roots that clutch. The artist in Communist countries is either an instrument of government propaganda, or is ostracized, like Pasternak and Solzhenitsyn. In the West, he is reduced to impotence or despair because of the refusal of society to listen to him unless he prostitutes himself to please the mass media and the lowest common denominator of taste.

Contrary to what some adverse critics have suggested, Eliot did not repudiate emotions and the capacity to feel, but he believed, as an artist, that emotions must not be paraded about, but fused into the work of art to the point where they reach universality and impersonality. "The first requisite usually held up by the promotors of personality is that a man should 'be himself'; and this 'sincerity' is considered more important than that the self in question should, socially and spiritually, be a good or a bad one." (*After Strange Gods*, p. 62.)

Eliot's poetry is studded with moments of extraordinary tension, all the more moving and memorable that they are expressed in strikingly precise imagery and in rhythms which, in spite of his lack of sympathy for the mellifluousness of Tennyson, or the surface music of Swinburne, combine, at times, the best of both. *La Figlia che Piange, Gerontion, Ash Wednesday, Marina, Journey of the Magi* and *Four Quartets*—perfect poetry of reconciliation and synthesis—testify to the strength of the poet's emotions and to his power to control them. And these strong emotions were also part of his life, but, discreet by nature, extremely sensitive as he was, he did not display them or allow them to be seen, unless they were part of a relationship which made them both natural and utterly private. One of the most intelligent poets of the twentieth century, he was, like Bertrand Russell, extremely wary of the use of the word "intellectual", and he carefully avoided intellectualism, in a poetry which is remarkable for its depth of thought and for the strength of his moral and religious convictions. He was extremely conscious in everything he did, for he felt very strongly that the poet is the consciousness of his time, which becomes aware of its true features through his work. And the poet can only be truly aware of his time if he sees his time as a continuation of what has taken place before, in the civilization to which he belongs. This implies the possession of an historical sense, and "the historical sense involves a perception, not only of the pastness of the past, but of its presence; the historical sense compels a man to write not merely with his own generation in his bones, but with a feeling that the whole of the literature of Europe from Homer and within it the whole of the literature of his own country has a simultaneous existence and composes a simultaneous order. This historical sense, which is a sense of the timeless as well as of the temporal and of the timeless and of the temporal together, is what makes a writer traditional. And it is at the same time what makes a writer most acutely conscious of his place in time, of his own contemporaneity." (*Selected Essays*, p. 14.)

Eliot has not only given our age a new poetic medium, he has also shown the way to an integrated artistic sensibility and attitude to life. He has understood that in an age of prose, "poetry must be as good and fluent as good prose". He has avoided the failings of some modernists, that is to say the use of technical terms in order to give an impression of modernity. Throughout his whole writing career, he has kept present in his mind Mallarmé's dictum: "Donner un sens plus pur aux mots de la tribu." He has made certain images and rhythms part of everyday life, and we cannot think of certain words, certain streets, passages, doorways, sunsets, fog, without recalling certain images from his poems. He has greatly contributed to the re-establishment of the long poem in English, and his attitude and technical influence is still evident in English poetry and drama from Auden and Larkin to Beckett and Pinter. His urgent concern for faith is certainly not present at the moment; but this does not detract in any way from his unique position in modern literature.

The aim of art is to reconnect the individual essence with the eternal essence. Art transmutes or renders apprehensible to the senses, truth which is always modified in its appearance, or shape, by the historic time or age to which it belongs, but remains unchanged at its core, which transcends time. A great work of art always transcends both time and the language or medium which embodies it, for the inspiration and the imagination which underlie it and which fuse it into oneness reach beyond time, to eternal essences. In order to understand or to grasp the cosmic analogies and relationships involved in such processes, one needs not only an historical imagination but also a metaphysical imagination. In spite of the fact that he was a very religious man, Eliot, who had a remarkable historical imagination, did not have the same range of metaphysical imagination as Yeats or Claudel, though he shared with them their basic interest in Eastern thought and their sense of history. But Eliot's naked sincerity and receptivity to growing experience— a growth which must not be denied to Yeats—give his poetry greater urgency and impact upon modern sensibility, and, together with the importance of his criticism, restore the balance. He is what Yeats and Claudel were not, at least not to the same extent—a great cosmopolitan writer. He not only tried to relate the Elizabethans to the metaphysicals and French Symbolism, Homer and Virgil to the poetry of Herbert, Blake and St. John of the Cross to the despair and sense of sin of Pascal and Baudelaire; he also tried to relate America to Europe as the fount and origin of Western civilization.

Eliot, American born, turned with the instinct of genius towards what he needed, in the same way in which Baudelaire had turned towards Poe. This is not a question of influence but of affinities, and Eliot himself has, it seems to me, put this point at its best in his essay on Massinger: "One of the surest of tests is the way in which a poet borrows. Immature poets imitate; mature poets steal; bad poets deface what they take, and good poets make it into something better, or at least something different. The good poet welds his theft into a whole of feeling which is unique, utterly different from that from which it was torn; the bad poet throws it into something which has no cohesion. A good poet will usually borrow from authors remote

155

in time, or alien in language, or diverse in interest. Chapman borrowed from Seneca; Shakespeare and Webster from Montaigne." (*Selected Essays*, p. 206.) Eliot was brought up in a climate in which American writers and teachers had established solid traditions of interest in European literature. He himself said: "The sense of the past was typically American", and he made serious studies of comparative literature which gave him a deep sense of the unity and interpenetrations of European culture. As the spiritual heir of Baudelaire, he is, like him, a European writer, for the simple reason that one could neither fully understand Europe without knowing his work, nor henceforth think of European thought and sensibility without thinking of the contribution he has made to it. With the exception of Goethe, who was quite conscious of his role as a great European, he is the one who, more than anyone else, has consciously, as well as subconsciously, contributed to the creation of artistic symbols which correspond to the European sensibility of his time. He achieved this important aim, not because, as some have suggested, he was lost at the cross-roads of Poe's and Whitman's poetry and was in search of a tradition, but because his genius enabled him to probe the depths of his European roots and to discover the dust and debris of a decaying world and the anxiety of fellow-beings lost in the lunar, lightless, waterless world of *The Waste Land*. The prosody and style of this poem correspond to its theme. A world which is no longer controlled by reason, a world adrift, barren and criss-crossed with illusions, could not be described in rhyming couplets or in stanzas of watertight logical precision. This kind of precision would have entailed a lack of psychological precision, and would only have been the Procrustean bed upon which fluctuating and imprecise psychological states and associations would have been stretched and turned into concepts. Only a musical structure, which, above all, respects the logic of sensibility, could attempt to follow and to suggest, through all sorts of fluid rhythms and affective associations of ideas and images, the fleeting vision of a world which has fallen to pieces and is without a centre, yet a world in which hope, though on the verge of total disappearance, is not completely dead.

## Conclusion

At the time when Eilot wrote *The Waste Land,* in spite of Arthur Symons's book on Symbolism and John Davidson's social awareness and urban imagery, and in spite of the fact that Bradley's subjectivism and William James's theories about consciousness were in the vanguard of European thought, the new sensibility, the synthesis of idealism and romanticism, as expressed in Symbolism, had not yet pervaded or had not been grasped by the English poetic genius. Baudelaire had been, according to Charles du Bos, "le premier en France à charger chaque mot du halo et de la frange des significations associées". Eliot did the same for the English language. Complexity of meaning, ambiguity and sensuous thought are part and parcel of great English poetry from Shakespeare to Shelley, but by the end of the nineteenth century and the beginning of the twentieth, poetry had shed its complexities and self-creativeness and was mostly a colourful cloak under which thoughts and sentiments were moving side by side, rarely meeting and, more often than not, dissolving in sentimentality. Living in an age in which the proletariat was assuming greater and greater importance, an age more and more dominated by the novel, that is to say by prose, Eliot realized, more acutely than most poets, the fact that poetic language had to come close to everyday speech, and that it was necessary to try to bring forth poetry not only out of specifically poetic themes and subjects but out of all the aspects and the complexities of everyday life. He has done for London what Baudelaire did for Paris, and he has left us unforgettable pictures of the life of this great city.

Certain critics and literary historians are inclined to construct compounds of diverse qualities and traits, abstracted from works of art, into criteria or models to which the works of other artists should thereafter conform. Thus, in such neatly compartmented worlds, we have not various traditions but one French tradition, one English tradition, one German tradition, etc., with all kinds of sub-traditions and counter-traditions, in arrangements which are as orderly and stiff as death itself. Shakespeare, Blake, Wordsworth, Lawrence and Yeats, for instance, are supposed to belong to the great English tradition.

whose governing regulations have been laid down by unhesi-
tating lawgivers and their followers, while Milton and Eliot are
not allowed to belong to such a tradition. The main reason why
Milton and Eliot are kept out of this tradition seems to be that
Milton read too much Latin and Italian and, like Eliot, is supposed to write English as if he were a foreigner. All this because Milton's prosody, which is the emanation of the structure
of his individuality and mind, is something which does not quite
correspond to the criteria which these critics use, and because
some of his cadences are also to be found in the Latin language.
As for Eliot, the fact that he came from America means for
these critics that he belongs to a country which had no poetic
tradition and that, therefore, he came to look for one in Europe.
Tradition seems to be something which poets put on, as judges
put on their wigs before going to court. Eliot certainly possessed
the mastery of a fully mature language, and he had genius; it
is difficult to see what else he needed.

With the integrity which is the hallmark of his work, he has
carefully and unflinchingly examined all the weaknesses and
sorrows which afflict men, and the solutions which he offers,
after protracted analyses and meditations, carry no trace of the
kind of facile optimism or of the cynical detachment which one
might find in anyone who tries to plumb the human heart without truly sharing its anxieties and sorrows. The solutions he
offers are those of a man who has never completely lost his
sense of the numinous and who, having accepted suffering and
calmly renounced all earthly hopes, has placed his faith in the
divine forgiveness in which he may find peace and eternal joy.

Eliot's world is a theocentric world, in which man and nature
are on the march towards their Maker, who has the two fundamental attributes of immanence and transcendence. On the
philosophical plane, this means that Time and Eternity are
again connected as they were in the Middle Ages by the instant,
which is the moment of Grace. The purely linear notion of Time
and of mechanistic rationalism has been replaced by the Bergsonian and Christian notions of Eternity and of the instant
which, in its fullness, fuses past and future into the present.
Human time is again the awareness that each human creature

has of the duration or moment of Grace which draws him out of nothingness, connects him with Being and reveals to him his essence. Knowledge is the past which is also the future lived in the present; thence the importance of the past, on the individual as well as on the national plane. Eliot followed the example of Dante, who took Virgil as a guide for his rise towards the summit. Like him, he felt the need of starting his journeys of discovery well fortified and supported by traditions which have deep roots in Europe. He is among those artists and thinkers whose names cannot be dissociated from that of Europe, and the survival of our civilization depends on our will to keep alive the values and the works which have truly contributed to the growth of man.

# BIBLIOGRAPHY

# BIBLIOGRAPHY

## I  Works by T. S. Eliot

(i) Published by Faber & Faber:

*Collected Poems, 1909–1962* (1969)
*Four Quartets* (1945)
*Poems written in Early Youth* (1967)
*The Cultivation of Christmas Trees* (1954)
*Old Possum's Book of Practical Cats* (1949)
*Collected Plays* (1969)—containing:
    *Murder in the Cathedral*
    *The Family Reunion*
    *The Cocktail Party*
    *The Confidential Clerk*
    *The Elder Statesman*
*Selected Essays* (1951)
*The Use of Poetry and the Use of Criticism* (1933)
*To Criticize the Critic* (1965)
*After Strange Gods* (1934)
*On Poetry and Poets* (1957)
*Elizabethan Dramatists* (1934)
*Dante* (1929)
*The Idea of a Christian Society* (1939)
*Notes towards the Definition of Culture* (1948)
*Knowledge and Experience in the Philosophy of F. H. Bradley*
    (1964)
*The Film of Murder in the Cathedral* (1942)
*Anabasis*—translation of a poem by St.-John Perse (1930)
*What is a Classic?* (1945)
*Essays Ancient and Modern* (1947)
*Introduction* to *A Choice of Kipling's Verse* (1941)
*Introduction* to *Selected Poems of Ezra Pound* (1928)
*Introduction* to *Literary Essays of Ezra Pound* (1954)
*Introduction* to *Introducing James Joyce* (1942)
*Preface* to Stanislaus Joyce: *My Brother's Keeper* (1957)
*Preface* to *Selected Poems of Edwin Muir*

160

## Bibliography

*Preface* to Anne Ridler: *A Little Book of Modern Verse* (1941)
*Preface* to Djuna Barnes: *Nightwood* (1937)
*The Waste Land*, facsimile and transcript, ed. Valerie Eliot (1971)

(ii) From other publishers:

*Selected Prose* (Penguin Books, 1953)
*From Poe to Valéry* (Harcourt Brace, 1948)
*The Sacred Wood* (Methuen, 1950)
*The Classic as a Man of Letters* (Oxford University Press, 1942)
*Christianity and Culture* (Harcourt Brace, 1940)
*Introduction* to Chiari, Joseph, *Contemporary French Poetry* (Manchester University Press, 1953)
*Introduction* to Chiari, Joseph, *From Poe to Mallarmé* (Barrie & Rockliff, 1956, and Gordian Press, New York, 1970)
*Introduction* to Knight, Wilson, *The Wheel of Fire* (Oxford University Press, 1930)

## II  A Selection of Critical Works on T. S. Eliot

Braybrooke, Neville, ed., *T. S. Eliot: A Symposium for his Seventieth Birthday* (London, 1958)
Browne, Martin, *The Making of T. S. Eliot's Plays* (Cambridge University Press, 1969)
Buckley, Vincent, *Poetry and Morality* (London, 1959)
Drew, Elizabeth, *T. S. Eliot, the Design of his Poetry* (Eyre & Spottiswoode, 1950)
Frye, Northrop, *T. S. Eliot* (Oliver & Boyd, 1963)
Gallup, D., *T. S. Eliot, a bibliography* (Faber and Harcourt Brace, 1952)
Gardner, Helen, *The Art of T. S. Eliot* (Cresset Press, 1949)
Grubb, Frederic, *A Vision of Reality* (Chatto & Windus, 1965)
Howarth, Herbert, *Notes on some Figures behind T. S. Eliot* (Chatto & Windus, 1965)
Jones, David, *The Plays of T. S. Eliot* (London, 1960)
Jones, Genesius, *Approach to the Purpose* (Hodder & Stoughton, 1963)
Kenner, Hugh, *The Invisible Poet: T. S. Eliot* (W. H. Allen, 1960)
Kenner, Hugh, ed., *T. S. Eliot, A Collection of Critical Essays* (New York, 1962)
March, Richard, ed., *T. S. Eliot, a Symposium* (London, 1948)

Matthiessen, F. O., *The Achievement of T. S. Eliot* (Oxford University Press, 1939; enlarged edition, 1947)

Maxwell, D. E. S., *Poetry of T. S. Eliot* (Routledge & Kegan Paul, 1961)

Preston, Raymond, *Four Quartets rehearsed* (London, 1946)

Ryan, B., ed., *T. S. Eliot, A Collection of Essays by Several Hands* (Dobson, 1947)

Smidt, Kristian, *Poetry and Belief in the work of T. S. Eliot* (Routledge & Kegan Paul, 1961)

Smith, Grover, *T. S. Eliot's Poetry and Plays: A Study in Sources and Meaning* (Chicago University Press, 1956)

Tate, Allen, ed., *T. S. Eliot, the Man and his Work* (Chatto & Windus, 1967)

Unger, Leonard, *T. S. Eliot, Moments and Patterns* (Manchester University Press, 1966)

— ed., *T. S. Eliot, A Selected Critique* (New York, 1948)

Williamson, George, *A Reader's Guide to T. S. Eliot* (London and New York, 1955)

Wilson, F. A. C. C., *Six Essays on the Development of T. S. Eliot* (London and New York, 1948)

# INDEX

# INDEX

# Index

Frazer, Sir James, 63, 148
Freud, Sigmund, 26, 148
Froude, J. A., 68
Fry, Christopher, 122

Gallup, Donald, 58
*Game of Chess, A, (Waste Land* II), 63–6, 69
Gautier, Théophile, 44, 46, 52, 54
Genius, scope of, 13
Georgian poets, 16, 17, 21, 23, 37, 117
*Gerontion*, 33, 46–51, 54, 58, 106–7, 153
Gide, André, 144
Gilbert, W. S., 11
Giraudoux, Jean, 118
Goethe, Johann W. von, 18, 31, 150, 156
Great War, 17, 23, 34, 48, 59
Greek drama, influence of, 111, 133–6
Guinicelli, Guido, 25

Halévy, Ludovic, 11
Hardy, Thomas, 16–18
Harvard University, 15, 18–19, 22, 30, 34, 44
Hegel, G. W. F., 19, 30, 103, 145, 148–9
Hemingway, Ernest, 19
Heraclitus, 31, 39, 85, 92, 104
Herbert, George, 155
Herrick, Robert, 17
Hinduism, 144
*Hippopotamus, The*, 52, 54
Hitler, Adolf, 35
Hobbes, Thomas, 13
Holland, 13, 48
*Hollow Men, The*, 71–4, 104, 145
Homer, 20, 154–5
Hopkins, Gerard Manley, 16, 18, 117
Hugo, Victor, 75
Hulme, T. E., 26
Hume, David, 15, 25
Huxley, T. H., 53

Ibsen, Henrik, 115, 119, 141
Imagism in poetry, 25–6
Impressionism, impressionists, 15, 30, 148
Internal monologue, use of, 26
Ivan the Terrible, 34

James, Henry, 19
James, William, 26, 157

John the Baptist, St., 40
John of the Cross, St., 77, 79, 93, 104, 110, 126, 144, 155
Johnson, Dr. Samuel, 147
*Journey of the Magi*, 105–7, 145, 153
Joyce, James, 19, 26, 57, 148
Julian of Norwich, 104
Jung, Carl Gustav, 148

Kandinsky, Vasili, 19
Kant, Immanuel, 30–2
Kenner, Hugh, *The Invisible Poet: T. S. Eliot*, 59, 111n.
Kierkegaard, Søren, 102–3
Kipling, Rudyard, 16, 33
Klee, Paul, 85
Knopf, Alfred, 53
Krishna, 104
Kyd, Thomas, *Spanish Tragedy*, 71

Laforgue, Jules, 15, 19–23, 44–5; *Autres Complaintes de Lord Pierrot*, 22, *L'Hiver qui vient*, 22; *Sombres Dimanches*, 21–2
La Goulue, 11
Lamartine, Alphonse de, 24
Larkin, Philip, 154
La Rochefoucauld, François, 46
Latini, Brunetto, 100
Lawrence, D. H., 16–18, 157
Leicester, Earl of, 68
Leopardi, Giacomo, 21
Lewis, C. Day, 18
*Little Gidding (Quartets* IV), 26, 91, 98–102, 104, 145, 148
*Little Review, The*, 53
Little Tich, 110
Lloyd, Marie, 11, 57, 110
Locke, John, 15, 25, 32
London, 71, 89–90, 100, 157
*Love Song of J. Alfred Prufrock*, 21, 36–41, 43, 47, 53, 81
Lucretius, *De Rerum Natura*, 27–8
*Lune de Miel* (Eliot), 54
Lyly, John, 64

Malherbe, François de, 93
Mallarmé, Stephane, 11, 15, 17–18, 30, 39, 53, 90, 100, 154; *L'Après-Midi d'un Faune*, 47; *Surgi de la croupe et du bond*, 64
*Marina*, 104, 107–10
Marlowe, Christopher, 49
Marsh, Edward, 16
Marvell, Andrew, 40, 55, 66
Marx, Karl, 149, 152

165

# Index

# Index